Overlay Networking: VXLAN, NVGRE and GENEVE in Virtual Networks

James Relington

DEDICATION

To those who seek knowledge, inspiration, and new perspectives—
may this book be a companion on your journey, a spark for curiosity,
and a reminder that every page turned is a step toward discovery.

AKNOWLEDGEMENTS

I would like to express my deepest gratitude to everyone who contributed to the creation of this book. To my colleagues and mentors, your insights and expertise have been invaluable. A special thank you to my family and friends for their unwavering support and encouragement throughout this journey.

Introduction to Overlay Networking

Overlay networking has emerged as a transformative paradigm in modern data center and cloud environments, addressing the growing complexity and scalability limitations of traditional networking architectures. As organizations increasingly adopt virtualization and distributed application models, the need for more agile, scalable, and flexible networking solutions has driven the development of overlay technologies. Overlay networking enables the creation of virtual networks that are logically decoupled from the underlying physical infrastructure, allowing for dynamic provisioning of network services across diverse and geographically dispersed environments. At its core, overlay networking introduces an abstraction layer on top of the existing physical network, encapsulating packets with additional headers to form tunnels between endpoints. These virtual tunnels allow hosts and virtual machines to communicate as if they were on the same Layer 2 or Layer 3 network, regardless of their actual location in the underlying physical topology.

This separation of concerns between the underlay and overlay layers is a key advantage, as it allows network administrators to implement new network designs and services without making disruptive changes to the physical network. For example, in traditional VLAN-based networks, scaling beyond a few thousand tenants becomes impractical due to the 12-bit VLAN ID limitation. Overlay technologies like VXLAN, NVGRE, and GENEVE overcome this limitation by using larger identifiers that support millions of unique segments, enabling scalable multi-tenant environments. This scalability is particularly critical in cloud data centers, where hundreds or thousands of tenants may need isolated networking resources. Overlay networking facilitates this by allowing the creation of virtual segments that can be dynamically assigned and managed independently of the physical topology.

In addition to scalability, overlay networking also enhances flexibility and mobility. In virtualized environments, workloads are often moved across physical hosts for load balancing, maintenance, or disaster recovery purposes. Overlay networks maintain consistent network policies and addressing as virtual machines move, ensuring uninterrupted connectivity and security. This capability supports a more agile and responsive infrastructure, aligned with the needs of modern application delivery models. For example, in a cloud environment, an application component may be dynamically scaled across multiple hosts, and overlay networking ensures that all instances remain part of the same logical network, regardless of where they are instantiated.

Security is another important consideration in overlay networking. By logically segmenting tenant networks, overlays enforce strong isolation between different customer environments or application tiers. Additionally, advanced features such as micro-segmentation and security policy enforcement can be integrated into the overlay control plane, allowing for fine-grained access control at the virtual network level. This is especially valuable in environments where traditional perimeter-based security models fall short, and where zero trust principles are increasingly being adopted.

The adoption of overlay networking is also closely tied to the rise of software-defined networking, or SDN. In SDN architectures, the control plane is decoupled from the data plane, enabling centralized network policy management and dynamic provisioning of network paths. Overlay networks leverage this separation by using software controllers to manage the mapping between virtual endpoints and physical network locations. These controllers maintain a database of tunnel endpoints, MAC and IP address mappings, and forwarding policies, allowing for rapid convergence and automated configuration of the network. This model significantly reduces the operational complexity associated with traditional networking, where each switch and router must be individually configured and managed.

Overlay networking protocols such as VXLAN, NVGRE, and GENEVE differ in their implementation details, but they all share the fundamental goal of enabling scalable, flexible, and automated virtual networking. VXLAN, for example, is widely adopted due to its simplicity, interoperability, and support from major hardware vendors. It uses UDP encapsulation and supports up to 16 million logical networks. NVGRE, developed by Microsoft, is integrated into Windows Server and Hyper-V environments and provides a similar tunneling mechanism using GRE encapsulation. GENEVE, on the other hand, is a newer and more extensible protocol designed to unify the best features of VXLAN and NVGRE while introducing a more flexible metadata format for future-proofing network services.

The transition to overlay networking also reflects a broader trend in IT toward abstraction and automation. Just as compute and storage have been virtualized and abstracted from physical hardware, networking is now undergoing a similar transformation. This enables faster deployment cycles, more consistent policy enforcement, and greater agility in responding to business needs. Overlay networking supports the vision of infrastructure as code, where networks are programmatically defined, deployed, and managed using orchestration tools and APIs. This shift not only improves operational efficiency but also opens the door to new capabilities such as intent-based networking and AI-driven network optimization.

However, overlay networking is not without its challenges. Visibility and troubleshooting can be more complex, as network packets are encapsulated and may not be easily inspected using traditional tools. Performance considerations also come into play, as encapsulation adds overhead and may impact throughput or latency in certain scenarios. To address these challenges, vendors have developed enhanced telemetry and analytics tools that provide deeper insight into overlay behavior, as well as hardware offloading features that accelerate encapsulation and decapsulation processes.

Overlay networking represents a foundational shift in the way networks are designed and operated in the era of cloud computing, virtualization, and distributed applications. By abstracting network services from physical constraints, it empowers organizations to build more scalable, secure, and dynamic environments that can adapt to the fast-changing demands of the digital landscape. As technologies and use cases continue to evolve, overlay networking will remain a critical enabler of innovation and agility in data center and cloud infrastructures.

The Evolution of Data Center Networks

The transformation of data center networks over the past several decades has been both profound and necessary, driven by the explosive growth in data, the emergence of cloud computing, and the shift toward virtualization and distributed applications. In the earliest days of enterprise computing, data centers were relatively simple environments, built around mainframes and directly attached storage. Networking in those environments was basic, often limited to point-to-point connections or rudimentary local area networks. As client-server computing emerged in the 1990s, the need for more structured and scalable networking grew, leading to the widespread adoption of Ethernet and the hierarchical three-tier network model consisting of access, aggregation, and core layers.

This model served traditional applications well, particularly those with predictable traffic patterns flowing north-south, meaning from the server to the user and back. These applications typically resided on a single physical server or at most required limited communication between a small number of hosts. Network design focused on reliability, redundancy, and deterministic paths. Switches and routers were purpose-built, and the management of these devices was largely manual, with configurations applied individually via command-line interfaces. Security policies, quality of service settings, and segmentation strategies were rigid and closely tied to physical topology. VLANs and subnets were used to group resources, but their scalability was limited and required careful planning to avoid overlapping address spaces and configuration conflicts.

As server virtualization began to take hold in the early 2000s, the foundations of traditional network design started to show signs of strain. With technologies like VMware and later Microsoft Hyper-V, it became possible to run multiple virtual machines on a single physical host, each with its own operating system, network stack, and application workloads. This drastically increased the density and dynamism of data center environments. Virtual machines could be provisioned or decommissioned in minutes, introducing a level of agility that traditional networks were not designed to support. The traffic patterns also began to change, with more east-west traffic—traffic flowing between virtual machines within the data center—taking precedence over north-south flows. Traditional hierarchical networks were not optimized for this shift, leading to bottlenecks and increased latency.

To adapt, data centers began to flatten their network topologies. The rise of leaf-spine architectures, in which each leaf switch connects to every spine switch, provided consistent latency and greater bandwidth across the fabric. This design reduced the number of hops between endpoints and improved the scalability of the network. However, even with more advanced physical architectures, the network still lacked the flexibility of the compute and storage layers. Every time a virtual machine moved from one host to another, especially across different Layer 3 subnets, the network had to be reconfigured to maintain connectivity and policy enforcement. These manual interventions were time-consuming and error-prone, creating friction in operations and slowing down application delivery.

The emergence of cloud computing further accelerated the need for more dynamic and programmable networks. Public cloud providers like Amazon Web Services, Microsoft Azure, and Google Cloud Platform offered users the ability to spin up thousands of virtual machines and containers on demand, all while managing network connectivity, security, and scaling automatically behind the scenes. Enterprises seeking to replicate these benefits in their own data centers quickly realized that traditional network designs were inadequate. The static nature of VLANs, the limited number of available network IDs, and the reliance on manual configuration created barriers to scalability and agility. Additionally, as more applications adopted microservices and distributed architectures, the need for fast and seamless communication between components became paramount.

This changing landscape gave rise to software-defined networking and overlay technologies. Software-defined networking introduced the concept of decoupling the control plane from the data plane, allowing centralized controllers to program network behavior dynamically. Overlay networks built on top of this principle by creating virtual networks that could span across the underlying physical infrastructure without being limited by its constraints. These overlays used encapsulation techniques to carry tenant or application-specific traffic over the underlay, effectively creating logical topologies that could be redefined and reconfigured in real time. VXLAN, NVGRE, and later GENEVE were developed as encapsulation protocols specifically designed to support this new model, enabling scalable multi-tenant environments with isolated broadcast domains and dynamic mobility.

With overlay networking, data center networks evolved from static, hardware-bound configurations to flexible, software-driven systems. This transition enabled automation, orchestration, and integration with broader IT management frameworks. Infrastructure as code became a reality, allowing network configurations to be version-controlled, audited, and deployed using the same tools and methodologies as software development. Policies could be defined based on identity, application, or intent, rather than IP addresses or VLAN tags. Network telemetry improved as well, with advanced analytics and visibility tools providing real-time insights into traffic flows, performance, and potential issues.

Another major milestone in the evolution of data center networks was the adoption of containers and orchestration platforms like Kubernetes. Containers brought a new level of agility and density, with lifespans measured in seconds or minutes rather than days or weeks. Networking had to adapt once again, supporting rapid provisioning, service discovery, and secure communication between ephemeral workloads. This led to the development of container networking interfaces and service meshes, which abstracted networking even further and provided built-in load balancing, encryption, and policy enforcement at the application layer.

Throughout this evolution, the fundamental goal of data center networking has remained the same: to connect workloads securely, efficiently, and reliably. What has changed is the scale, speed, and complexity of the environments in which these workloads operate. From static mainframes to dynamic cloud-native applications, data center networks have had to reinvent themselves to meet new demands. The journey has been marked by innovation in both hardware and software, with an increasing emphasis on programmability, automation, and integration with broader IT ecosystems. Overlay networking now sits at the center of this evolution, providing the foundation for modern network virtualization and enabling the flexible, scalable, and tenant-aware infrastructures that today's digital enterprises require.

Traditional VLAN Limitations

Virtual Local Area Networks, or VLANs, have played a central role in network segmentation and traffic isolation for decades. They were introduced as a solution to overcome the physical limitations of flat Layer 2 networks by allowing multiple logical networks to exist on the same physical infrastructure. This innovation made it possible to group devices by function or department, regardless of their physical location, and to control broadcast domains more efficiently. However, as networks have grown in complexity and scale—especially in virtualized and cloud-based environments—several inherent limitations of traditional VLANs have become increasingly evident. These limitations have prompted the industry to seek more flexible, scalable, and dynamic alternatives to meet modern networking demands.

One of the most fundamental constraints of VLANs lies in their scalability. VLANs are identified by a 12-bit VLAN ID field in the IEEE 802.1Q header, which allows for a maximum of 4096 unique VLANs per network. While this might seem sufficient for smaller environments, it quickly becomes a bottleneck in large-scale data centers, multi-tenant environments, and cloud service providers, where each tenant or application might require its own isolated network segment. In these scenarios, thousands of isolated segments are not just preferred—they are necessary for ensuring security, compliance, and operational separation. The 4096 VLAN limit, therefore, acts as a hard ceiling that prevents networks from scaling to meet the needs of dynamic, service-rich environments.

Another significant limitation of VLANs is their dependence on Layer 2 broadcast domains. In a VLAN-based network, all devices in the same VLAN are part of the same broadcast domain, meaning that broadcasts sent by one device are received by all others in that VLAN. As the number of devices in a VLAN increases, so does the volume of broadcast traffic, which can lead to network congestion and degraded performance. This broadcast dependency is particularly problematic in virtualized environments, where hundreds or thousands of virtual machines may exist on a single VLAN. The broadcast storms that can result from this architecture pose a threat to network stability and make it difficult to scale the network effectively.

Mobility of workloads is another area where VLANs fall short. In virtualized data centers, virtual machines are frequently moved between physical hosts for load balancing, maintenance, or scaling purposes. For a virtual machine to retain its network identity and connectivity during such a move, the destination host must be part of the same VLAN. This requirement often forces network administrators to stretch VLANs across the data center, creating Layer 2 links that span multiple switches and potentially multiple locations. Stretching VLANs in this manner increases complexity, introduces potential for loops, and can lead to issues with convergence and troubleshooting. It also tightly couples network design to the physical infrastructure, limiting the agility of operations and making it more difficult to implement efficient, modular architectures.

Traditional VLANs also present challenges in terms of operational complexity. Network changes involving VLANs typically require manual configuration of switches, routers, and access control policies. Each time a new VLAN is needed, administrators must configure VLAN IDs, assign ports, and ensure consistency across the network fabric. This manual process is time-consuming, error-prone, and does not scale well with the speed of modern IT operations. Furthermore, VLAN-based segmentation relies on static mappings, which do not adapt to changing conditions or dynamically adjust to workload demands. In environments where automation, orchestration, and policy-based control are essential, VLANs represent a rigid and outdated model.

Security is another area where VLANs show their limitations. While VLANs provide a basic level of isolation between network segments, they are not inherently secure. Misconfigurations, VLAN hopping attacks, and insufficient access control measures can expose sensitive data and create vulnerabilities. In environments that demand fine-grained segmentation, such as those adhering to zero trust principles or handling sensitive workloads, VLANs alone are not sufficient to enforce security policies. They lack the ability to apply context-aware rules based on user identity, application type, or device posture. Instead, they rely solely on IP addressing and port-level controls, which are increasingly inadequate in dynamic, multi-cloud, and hybrid environments.

Another critical issue with VLANs is their poor fit with multi-tenancy. In cloud data centers and service provider environments, multiple tenants must coexist on the same physical infrastructure while maintaining strict isolation. Each tenant may require its own network topology, security policies, and routing configurations. With only 4096 VLANs available and no support for tenant-specific metadata or dynamic network constructs, VLANs cannot adequately support these requirements. Workarounds such as using separate VRFs or additional encapsulation layers add complexity and reduce manageability, further highlighting the inadequacy of traditional VLANs in supporting modern service delivery models.

The integration of VLANs with virtual networking components also presents limitations. In hypervisor-based environments, virtual switches operate alongside physical switches, and coordinating VLAN assignments across these layers becomes challenging. Misalignments between virtual and physical configurations can result in dropped packets, asymmetric routing, or degraded performance. Moreover, VLANs do not inherently support programmability or integration with software-defined networking controllers, limiting their usefulness in automated and orchestrated environments. They were designed for a static, hardware-centric world and struggle to operate efficiently in dynamic, software-defined infrastructures.

Even interoperability can be an issue in VLAN-based networks. Different vendors may implement VLAN tagging and trunking in slightly different ways, and proprietary enhancements can lead to compatibility issues when integrating multi-vendor environments. Additionally, managing VLANs across different geographic locations or administrative domains requires significant coordination and increases the likelihood of configuration drift. This lack of consistency makes it difficult to scale VLANs across distributed data centers or hybrid cloud environments.

As networking requirements continue to evolve toward greater agility, scalability, and automation, the limitations of traditional VLANs become more apparent. They were an important step in the evolution of network segmentation, but they were never designed to meet the demands of large-scale, virtualized, and multi-tenant architectures. Their rigid structure, limited scalability, and reliance on static, manually configured parameters make them ill-suited to the dynamic, policy-driven environments that define modern data center and cloud networks. For these reasons, the industry has increasingly turned to overlay networking technologies and software-defined approaches to overcome the constraints imposed by VLANs and to enable the next generation of network virtualization.

Overlay Networking Concepts and Terminology

Overlay networking introduces a powerful abstraction layer in modern data center and cloud environments, enabling the decoupling of logical network topologies from the underlying physical infrastructure. This approach allows for unprecedented levels of scalability, agility, and flexibility by encapsulating traffic into tunnels that span across a physical network, known as the underlay. Through this encapsulation, overlay networks create isolated virtual environments where communication between workloads can occur independently of their physical location, promoting mobility and dynamic resource allocation. To fully understand how overlay networking operates and why it is fundamental to modern network architectures, it is essential to examine the key concepts and terminology that underpin it.

At the heart of overlay networking is the notion of abstraction. Unlike traditional network models, where topology and addressing are tightly coupled to physical devices, overlays allow network architects to define virtual topologies based on operational or application requirements rather than physical constraints. These topologies are constructed using tunnels—virtual paths between endpoints—across the underlay. The underlay is typically composed of high-speed IP-based networks that focus on delivering packets from one point to another without needing awareness of the overlay's structure. The overlay, on the other hand, is built on top of this physical infrastructure and uses encapsulation techniques to package data in a format that allows it to traverse the underlay while maintaining the logical separation required by virtual networks.

Encapsulation is a foundational concept in overlay networking. It refers to the process of adding a header to each packet, allowing it to be treated as payload by the underlay. This new header contains information required to route the packet to its destination overlay endpoint, where it is decapsulated and delivered to the appropriate virtual machine or container. This model enables multiple isolated virtual networks to coexist on the same physical infrastructure without interference. Overlay protocols such as VXLAN, NVGRE, and GENEVE implement different encapsulation formats, each designed to meet specific scalability and extensibility requirements.

Tunnel Endpoints are another critical concept in overlay networks. These are the devices, often virtual switches or physical NICs with tunneling capabilities, that perform the encapsulation and decapsulation of overlay traffic. A tunnel endpoint at the source will encapsulate a packet with an appropriate overlay header and forward it across the underlay. The receiving endpoint will remove the overlay header and deliver the packet to the correct virtual interface. These endpoints maintain mappings of virtual network identifiers to physical addresses, which are necessary to ensure that packets reach their correct destinations. In software-defined networking environments, these mappings are often managed by a centralized control plane.

The separation of control plane and data plane is also a defining characteristic of overlay networking. The control plane is responsible for managing the state of the network, such as maintaining endpoint mappings, policies, and forwarding rules. The data plane, by contrast, is concerned with the actual forwarding of packets based on the instructions provided by the control plane. In overlay architectures, the control plane can be centralized, as seen in SDN environments, or distributed, depending on the design and scale of the deployment. Centralized control planes provide simplified management and a global view of the network, while distributed models offer greater resiliency and scalability.

Overlay networks rely heavily on identifiers to distinguish between different virtual networks. The most common identifier used is the Virtual Network Identifier, or VNI, in the case of VXLAN. The VNI is a 24-bit field that allows for over 16 million unique logical segments, far surpassing the 4096 VLAN limit in traditional Ethernet networks. Each virtual network is assigned a unique VNI, ensuring complete isolation of traffic. This identifier is embedded in the overlay header and allows tunnel endpoints to direct traffic to the appropriate virtual switch or interface. Other protocols, such as NVGRE and GENEVE, use similar identifiers to achieve the same goal of scalable segmentation.

Isolation is a central principle in overlay networking. Each virtual network created within an overlay is completely isolated from the others, allowing for secure multi-tenancy and granular policy enforcement. This isolation extends beyond just Layer 2 domains and can be implemented across Layer 3 as well, depending on the protocol and control plane used. By isolating tenants or applications, overlay networking enables compliance with strict security standards and supports diverse use cases, from enterprise data centers to public cloud platforms.

East-west and north-south traffic flows take on new meaning in overlay environments. East-west traffic, referring to communication between workloads within the same data center, is highly optimized by overlay networks due to their flat, logical topology. North-south traffic, which moves between the data center and external networks, can also be efficiently handled by integrating overlay gateways that translate between overlay and traditional routing domains. This architecture enables seamless communication between legacy systems and modern virtualized workloads.

Overlay networks also introduce the concept of dynamic provisioning. With the integration of orchestration platforms and software-defined controls, virtual networks can be created, modified, or deleted on demand. This level of programmability allows networks to adapt in real-time to changing workloads, user demands, and application requirements. APIs and automation tools can be used to provision overlay networks as part of larger service deployment workflows, enabling true infrastructure-as-code practices.

In addition to scalability and flexibility, overlay networks provide enhanced mobility. Because the logical network is decoupled from the physical topology, virtual machines and containers can be moved across the infrastructure without needing to reconfigure the network. The tunnel endpoints automatically update their mappings and forwarding rules, ensuring uninterrupted connectivity and consistent policy enforcement. This mobility is particularly valuable in environments that utilize live migration, load balancing, or auto-scaling features.

Visibility and monitoring in overlay networks require advanced tools capable of interpreting encapsulated traffic. Traditional network monitoring tools often fail to provide meaningful insights into overlay traffic because they do not recognize or decode the encapsulated headers. Modern visibility platforms integrate with the control plane and use deep packet inspection, telemetry data, and flow analytics to deliver comprehensive views of overlay performance and health. These tools are essential for diagnosing issues, ensuring compliance, and optimizing performance.

Overlay networking represents a shift from static, hardware-bound configurations to fluid, software-defined environments. By understanding the core concepts of abstraction, encapsulation, tunnel endpoints, identifiers, control and data planes, and dynamic provisioning, network engineers can harness the full potential of overlays to build resilient, scalable, and agile infrastructures. As cloud adoption and virtualization continue to reshape IT landscapes, mastery of overlay networking terminology and architecture becomes not just beneficial but essential.

The Role of Tunneling in Modern Networks

Tunneling has become a fundamental technique in the architecture of modern networks, enabling the creation of virtual communication paths over existing physical infrastructure. This capability has been instrumental in supporting the demands of virtualization, cloud computing, multi-tenancy, and network abstraction. By encapsulating packets within other packets, tunneling allows data to traverse incompatible or complex networks while maintaining the integrity, isolation, and identity of the original traffic. This approach has radically transformed how networks are built, managed, and scaled, and its role continues to expand as IT infrastructures become more distributed and dynamic.

In traditional networking, devices and services communicated directly over a shared infrastructure, with clear visibility into each packet's source and destination. This model worked well in simple, static environments where workloads were fixed and topologies rarely changed. However, as enterprises embraced server virtualization and moved toward highly dynamic environments, the limitations of physical network segmentation and address management became more pronounced. Virtual machines and containers began to move fluidly between physical hosts, creating a need for consistent connectivity and policy enforcement regardless of their location. Tunneling emerged as a solution to bridge these gaps by creating logical paths that could span across Layer 2 and Layer 3 boundaries without relying on rigid physical topology.

At its core, tunneling involves encapsulating an original packet inside a new packet, adding a new header that provides routing information for the underlying transport network. The encapsulated packet travels across the underlay infrastructure, which is unaware of the payload's contents or its final destination within the overlay network. Once the packet reaches its endpoint, the tunneling header is stripped away, and the original packet is forwarded as if it had traveled directly. This mechanism allows for the creation of virtual networks that are isolated, scalable, and portable, offering network designers a high degree of flexibility and control.

The use of tunneling in data center networks has grown rapidly alongside the adoption of network virtualization technologies. Protocols such as Virtual Extensible LAN (VXLAN), Network Virtualization using Generic Routing Encapsulation (NVGRE), and Generic Network Virtualization Encapsulation (GENEVE) all rely on tunneling to establish overlay networks. These protocols enable the encapsulation of Ethernet frames within IP packets, allowing Layer 2 segments to be extended across Layer 3 infrastructure. This is particularly important in large-scale environments, where Layer 2 connectivity is required for legacy applications, VM mobility, or tenant isolation, but where traditional Layer 2 extension methods would be inefficient or operationally complex.

Tunneling plays a critical role in overcoming the scalability limitations of traditional VLANs. With protocols like VXLAN, which uses a 24-bit segment ID known as the VNI, networks can support up to 16 million isolated segments—far beyond the 4096 VLAN limit. This allows service providers and large enterprises to support thousands of tenants, each with their own isolated network, without running into resource constraints. These tunnels can also span across data centers or geographic locations, making it possible to build highly distributed and resilient architectures that still operate as cohesive logical networks.

Another major advantage of tunneling is its support for mobility. When a virtual machine or container moves from one host to another, its IP address and network identity can remain unchanged as long as the overlay network is intact. The tunnel endpoints automatically adjust to the new location, updating their forwarding tables and ensuring seamless connectivity. This mobility is crucial in environments that use dynamic orchestration platforms, such as Kubernetes or OpenStack, where workloads are frequently scaled or migrated based on demand. Tunneling ensures that network policies, access controls, and service connectivity follow the workload, reducing the need for manual reconfiguration or complex routing adjustments.

Security is also enhanced through the use of tunneling. By encapsulating traffic and transmitting it over isolated tunnels, networks can enforce strict segmentation between tenants, departments, or application tiers. This isolation minimizes the risk of lateral movement by malicious actors and provides a clear boundary between environments. When combined with encryption at the tunnel layer, such as using IPsec or DTLS, tunneling can also protect data in transit from eavesdropping or tampering. These features are especially valuable in hybrid cloud or multi-cloud deployments, where traffic may traverse shared or untrusted infrastructure.

Despite its many benefits, tunneling introduces new operational considerations. The added encapsulation increases packet size, which can lead to issues with MTU (Maximum Transmission Unit) if the underlying network is not properly configured to handle larger frames. Fragmentation or packet drops may occur if tunnel headers push packets beyond the supported MTU, resulting in performance degradation or connectivity problems. To address this, network operators must ensure that the underlay supports jumbo frames or that appropriate path MTU discovery mechanisms are in place.

Visibility and monitoring also become more complex in tunneled environments. Traditional network tools that inspect packet headers may be unable to interpret encapsulated traffic, making it harder to diagnose problems or monitor flows. As a result, modern overlay networks often require specialized telemetry systems and analytics platforms capable of decoding tunnel headers and correlating overlay traffic with physical network performance. These tools are essential for maintaining operational awareness, detecting anomalies, and ensuring service-level objectives are met.

The performance impact of tunneling is another area that demands attention. Although software-based tunnel endpoints offer great flexibility, they may introduce CPU overhead if not offloaded to specialized hardware. To mitigate this, many modern NICs and switches support tunneling offload, allowing encapsulation and decapsulation tasks to be handled in silicon. This approach improves throughput, reduces latency, and frees up compute resources for application workloads. When designing a network architecture that relies heavily on tunneling, it is essential to consider hardware support and align performance expectations accordingly.

Tunneling has become an essential component of network design in modern infrastructures, providing the foundation for overlay networking, multi-tenancy, mobility, and secure segmentation. Its ability to abstract physical constraints and enable logical connectivity makes it a powerful tool for network architects, especially in environments where agility, scalability, and automation are critical. As organizations continue to embrace cloud-native technologies, hybrid architectures, and software-defined models, tunneling will remain at the core of how networks are built, operated, and evolved.

Encapsulation Techniques Overview

Encapsulation techniques serve as the foundational mechanisms behind overlay networking, enabling the transport of packets across logical networks that are decoupled from the underlying physical infrastructure. These techniques allow original Ethernet or IP packets to be wrapped with an additional protocol header, effectively creating a tunnel that carries the payload from one endpoint to another across an existing network. By hiding the complexity of the transport network and preserving the identity and context of the original traffic, encapsulation provides a method to achieve scalability, isolation, and flexibility in modern network architectures. As network environments have grown more virtualized, containerized, and distributed, the importance of encapsulation has increased, giving rise to several encapsulation protocols specifically designed to address the needs of overlay networking.

One of the primary goals of encapsulation is to enable the creation of virtual networks that operate independently of the physical topology. This abstraction is essential in multi-tenant data centers, cloud environments, and software-defined networks where workloads are dynamic and often mobile. By encapsulating each packet with a protocol-specific header that includes routing and identification information, the network can forward traffic across a physical infrastructure without requiring awareness of the virtual network's internal structure. This is especially useful for preserving Layer 2 adjacency across Layer 3 boundaries, maintaining consistent policy enforcement, and supporting live migration of virtual machines or containers.

The encapsulation process typically involves taking an Ethernet or IP packet and enclosing it within a new IP packet that includes a tunneling header. The tunneling header contains critical information such as the virtual network identifier, source and destination tunnel endpoints, and sometimes additional metadata used for policy enforcement, segmentation, or telemetry. When the encapsulated packet reaches the destination endpoint, the tunneling header is stripped away, and the original packet is delivered to its intended recipient. This approach ensures that the packet travels through the network with minimal disruption to its content while allowing for complete control over its path and behavior.

Several encapsulation protocols have been developed to support overlay networking, each with its own structure, capabilities, and intended use cases. Among the most widely adopted are Virtual Extensible LAN (VXLAN), Network Virtualization using Generic Routing Encapsulation (NVGRE), and Generic Network Virtualization Encapsulation (GENEVE). Each of these protocols builds upon earlier tunneling methods such as GRE and MPLS, adding enhancements that make them more suitable for highly virtualized and dynamic environments.

VXLAN is perhaps the most commonly used encapsulation protocol in overlay networking today. Developed by VMware, Cisco, and Arista, VXLAN was designed to overcome the limitations of traditional VLANs, specifically their lack of scalability and flexibility. VXLAN encapsulates Layer 2 Ethernet frames within UDP packets, allowing them to be transported across standard IP networks. One of its key features is the use of a 24-bit VXLAN Network Identifier, or VNI, which supports up to 16 million unique virtual networks—far surpassing the 4096 limit imposed by VLAN IDs. VXLAN operates using tunnel endpoints called VTEPs, or VXLAN Tunnel Endpoints, which are responsible for encapsulating and decapsulating traffic. Because VXLAN uses UDP for transport, it is compatible with existing IP routing infrastructure and can take advantage of ECMP (Equal-Cost

Multi-Path) routing to distribute traffic efficiently across multiple paths.

NVGRE, introduced by Microsoft, is another encapsulation technique designed to facilitate network virtualization, particularly in Windows Server and Hyper-V environments. NVGRE encapsulates Ethernet frames using GRE, or Generic Routing Encapsulation, and includes a 24-bit tenant network identifier embedded in the GRE key field. Like VXLAN, NVGRE aims to provide scalable isolation and tenant segmentation over Layer 3 networks. However, unlike VXLAN, which benefits from widespread vendor support and interoperability, NVGRE has seen more limited adoption outside the Microsoft ecosystem. Nevertheless, it serves as a critical reference point in the evolution of encapsulation protocols, influencing the design of later, more flexible standards.

GENEVE, developed by the IETF with contributions from VMware, Microsoft, and other major vendors, represents the next generation of encapsulation protocols. It was created to combine the strengths of VXLAN and NVGRE while adding extensibility as a core feature. GENEVE uses UDP as its transport protocol but introduces a highly flexible header format that includes support for variable-length options. These options allow network operators to attach metadata to each packet, such as policy tags, telemetry information, or quality-of-service indicators. This extensibility makes GENEVE well-suited for software-defined environments where programmability and adaptability are essential. GENEVE is designed to be future-proof, enabling the addition of new features without modifying the core protocol or breaking interoperability.

Despite their differences, all encapsulation techniques share the challenge of introducing additional overhead. Each tunneling header increases the size of the packet, potentially leading to issues with Maximum Transmission Unit (MTU) settings if the network is not configured to support jumbo frames. If packets exceed the MTU, they may be fragmented or dropped, resulting in performance degradation or connection problems. Therefore, careful planning and configuration are required to ensure that the physical infrastructure can handle the increased packet sizes introduced by encapsulation.

Another consideration is the impact on visibility and monitoring. Encapsulated traffic may bypass traditional monitoring tools that rely on inspecting standard headers, making it harder to diagnose issues or analyze flows. To address this, modern telemetry solutions must be capable of interpreting encapsulated packets and correlating overlay traffic with underlay performance. Some encapsulation protocols, particularly GENEVE, are designed with telemetry in mind and support mechanisms for embedding monitoring data directly into the packet header.

Encapsulation also interacts with hardware acceleration capabilities. Many modern network interface cards and switches support offloading of encapsulation and decapsulation tasks to dedicated hardware, improving performance and reducing the burden on host CPUs. These offload features are especially important in environments with high-throughput requirements, such as cloud data centers or high-performance computing clusters. Ensuring compatibility between encapsulation protocols and hardware capabilities is a crucial step in designing efficient and scalable overlay networks.

As networking continues to evolve toward software-defined and cloud-native models, encapsulation techniques will remain central to the design and operation of flexible, scalable infrastructures. Understanding the strengths, limitations, and use cases of protocols like VXLAN, NVGRE, and GENEVE provides network architects with the tools needed to build robust overlay networks capable of meeting the demands of modern applications and services. These encapsulation methods do not just transport data—they create the foundation for dynamic, programmable, and secure virtual networks that operate seamlessly across physical boundaries.

Introduction to VXLAN

Virtual Extensible LAN, or VXLAN, is a network virtualization technology that has become a cornerstone in the design of modern data centers and cloud infrastructures. It was developed as a solution to overcome the limitations of traditional VLANs and to support scalable, dynamic, and multi-tenant network architectures. As data centers evolved to include thousands of virtual machines and containers, the need for a more flexible and extensible overlay network became evident. VXLAN addresses this need by providing a way to encapsulate Layer 2 Ethernet frames within Layer 3 IP packets, enabling the creation of virtual Layer 2 networks across a Layer 3 infrastructure.

The rise of server virtualization and the increasing density of workloads on physical hosts introduced new challenges in data center networking. VLANs, which were once sufficient for segmenting traffic and providing basic isolation, became inadequate in environments requiring greater scalability and mobility. The 12-bit VLAN ID field only allows for 4096 unique VLANs, which is far too limited for large-scale, multi-tenant data centers. VXLAN resolves this constraint by introducing a 24-bit VXLAN Network Identifier, or VNI, which supports over 16 million unique segments. This expansion allows service providers and enterprises to assign a separate VNI to each tenant or application, providing complete traffic isolation and eliminating the risk of ID exhaustion.

The VXLAN architecture relies on a concept known as tunneling. It encapsulates Ethernet frames in User Datagram Protocol (UDP) packets, which are then transmitted over an IP network. This encapsulation allows the original Layer 2 traffic to traverse Layer 3 boundaries, effectively extending Layer 2 networks across different physical locations and network segments. VXLAN tunnels are established between devices called VXLAN Tunnel Endpoints, or VTEPs. These endpoints are responsible for performing encapsulation and decapsulation, translating the original Ethernet frames into VXLAN packets and vice versa. VTEPs can be implemented in virtual switches within hypervisors or in physical network devices, depending on the deployment model and architectural preferences.

One of the key advantages of VXLAN is its ability to work seamlessly over existing IP networks. Because VXLAN uses UDP as its transport protocol, it is fully compatible with the IP routing infrastructure that forms the backbone of modern data centers. This compatibility allows network operators to deploy VXLAN without requiring significant changes to their underlay networks. It also enables the use of Equal-Cost Multi-Path (ECMP) routing, which distributes traffic across multiple paths and enhances performance, fault tolerance, and bandwidth utilization. This is especially beneficial in spine-leaf architectures, where redundant links between switches can be efficiently leveraged to handle high volumes of east-west traffic.

The VXLAN header includes the VNI, which is used by the receiving VTEP to identify the target virtual network. The encapsulated packet carries the original Ethernet frame as payload, preserving the MAC addresses and other Layer 2 attributes. This preservation is critical for maintaining application compatibility and supporting features like ARP, broadcast, and multicast within the virtual network. However, unlike traditional Layer 2 networks, VXLAN enables these features to be implemented in a way that scales efficiently across large infrastructures.

Initially, VXLAN was implemented using a flood-and-learn mechanism, similar to traditional Ethernet. In this model, unknown destination MAC addresses and broadcast traffic are flooded across the VXLAN network, and each VTEP learns MAC address mappings by observing incoming traffic. While simple to implement, this approach does not scale well in large environments and can lead to excessive broadcast traffic. To address this limitation, VXLAN has evolved to support more sophisticated control plane mechanisms, such as Ethernet Virtual Private Network (EVPN). EVPN provides a BGP-based control plane that allows VTEPs to exchange MAC address and VNI mappings, eliminating the need for flooding and significantly improving scalability, convergence, and security.

The flexibility of VXLAN makes it suitable for a wide range of use cases. In multi-tenant cloud environments, VXLAN enables each tenant to have isolated virtual networks that span across the physical data center. In enterprise networks, VXLAN supports workload mobility, allowing virtual machines to move between hosts without requiring changes to IP addressing or security policies. In hybrid cloud scenarios, VXLAN can be used to extend on-premises networks into public cloud environments, creating a consistent and seamless network experience for applications and users.

VXLAN also plays an important role in supporting micro-segmentation, a security strategy that enforces fine-grained policies at the individual workload level. Because VXLAN allows for the creation of numerous isolated segments, it becomes easier to implement access controls and firewall policies that apply specifically to individual applications or tenants. This level of granularity is essential in zero trust architectures, where trust is not automatically granted based on network location but must be explicitly defined through policy.

Despite its advantages, deploying VXLAN requires careful planning and design. Network administrators must consider factors such as MTU size, as the addition of VXLAN headers increases packet size and may require adjustments to support jumbo frames. They must also account for the processing overhead associated with encapsulation and decapsulation, which can impact performance if not properly offloaded to hardware. Modern network interface cards and switches often include VXLAN offload capabilities to address this concern and ensure optimal performance.

Another consideration is visibility and troubleshooting. Because VXLAN traffic is encapsulated, traditional monitoring tools may not be able to inspect or analyze the contents of packets without additional capabilities. To address this, network visibility solutions must support VXLAN decoding and be integrated with the control plane to provide context-aware insights. These tools are critical for maintaining performance, diagnosing issues, and ensuring compliance in complex overlay environments.

VXLAN has become a critical enabler of scalable, flexible, and programmable networks. Its widespread adoption across both virtual and physical platforms reflects its ability to meet the demands of modern IT environments. By extending Layer 2 networks over IP, supporting massive scalability, and enabling dynamic workload mobility, VXLAN allows organizations to build network architectures that align with the speed, scale, and agility required by today's applications and services. Whether used in a private data center, a public cloud, or a hybrid deployment, VXLAN provides the foundational overlay that bridges the gap between traditional networking and the future of fully virtualized infrastructure.

VXLAN Header Structure

Understanding the VXLAN header structure is essential to grasp how Virtual Extensible LAN functions and delivers scalable network virtualization. The VXLAN header plays a pivotal role in encapsulating Layer 2 Ethernet frames within Layer 3 IP packets, enabling seamless connectivity across physically and geographically distributed networks. By wrapping original Ethernet frames with a well-defined header and leveraging UDP for transport, VXLAN creates a tunnel between endpoints known as VXLAN Tunnel Endpoints or VTEPs. These tunnels are the logical pathways that carry encapsulated traffic from one virtual network segment to another, maintaining tenant isolation, network identity, and policy consistency across the infrastructure.

The encapsulation process in VXLAN transforms a standard Ethernet frame into a VXLAN packet that can traverse an IP network. This transformation involves the addition of a VXLAN header, a UDP header, and outer IP and Ethernet headers. Each of these layers contributes specific fields and functions, but it is the VXLAN header itself that defines the logical segmentation and identifies the virtual network. The VXLAN header is inserted between the original Ethernet frame and the UDP header, making it a crucial part of the encapsulation scheme. It carries metadata that helps the receiving VTEP interpret and deliver the inner payload correctly.

The VXLAN header is an 8-byte structure that begins with a reserved field followed by several flags, then the VXLAN Network Identifier, or VNI. The reserved field is 8 bits long and is not used for any operational purpose; it is typically set to zero and reserved for future extensions or alignment purposes. Following the reserved field is an 8-bit flags section. This section contains various flags, but most importantly, it includes the I flag. The I flag is the only bit currently in active use, and it must be set to one to indicate that the VNI field is valid. If the I flag is not set, the packet is considered invalid, and the receiver should discard it. The remaining seven bits in the flags field are reserved and must be set to zero to maintain compatibility and prevent misinterpretation.

Next in the VXLAN header is a 24-bit field that holds the VXLAN Network Identifier. This field is the core element of the VXLAN header, as it defines the logical segment to which the encapsulated traffic belongs. With 24 bits available, the VNI supports more than 16 million unique identifiers. This large address space is a dramatic improvement over the 12-bit VLAN ID used in traditional Ethernet networks, which only allows for 4096 segments. Each VNI represents a separate virtual network, providing complete isolation between tenants or applications running in a multi-tenant data center. The VNI is assigned by the network control plane or configured manually, depending on the deployment model, and it is used by the receiving VTEP to identify the virtual network context in which the payload should be delivered.

Following the VNI is another 8-bit reserved field. Like the first reserved field, this section is not currently used and is set to zero. It exists primarily to maintain alignment and ensure that the VXLAN header conforms to expected structures across implementations. Although these reserved fields do not serve an active role, they provide flexibility for potential future enhancements to the protocol.

The VXLAN header is encapsulated inside a UDP packet, which itself includes a source port, destination port, length, and checksum. The destination port is typically set to 4789, which is the Internet Assigned Numbers Authority (IANA) designated port for VXLAN. This allows receiving devices to easily identify and process VXLAN packets. The source port is dynamically generated, often based on a hash of the inner packet headers. This dynamic source port selection provides entropy, which helps with load balancing across Equal-Cost Multi-Path routes in the underlay IP network. The length and checksum fields follow standard UDP format and help ensure that the packet is delivered correctly and intact.

Above the UDP header is the IP header, which provides routing information across the underlay network. The source and destination IP addresses in this header correspond to the IP addresses of the source and destination VTEPs. This layer ensures that the packet is routed across the Layer 3 infrastructure to its intended endpoint. Above the IP header is the outer Ethernet header, which is used to forward the packet within the physical Ethernet fabric. This header includes the MAC addresses of the physical network interfaces of the source and destination devices. Together, these outer headers encapsulate the VXLAN payload and provide the necessary information to traverse the physical network infrastructure.

When the VXLAN packet reaches its destination VTEP, the outer Ethernet, IP, and UDP headers are stripped away, and the VXLAN header is interpreted. The VNI is extracted to determine the target virtual network, and the original Ethernet frame is delivered to the appropriate virtual interface or virtual machine. This decapsulation process restores the original packet as if it had been transmitted within a traditional Layer 2 domain, preserving the expected behavior of the application or service.

The structure of the VXLAN header, while compact, encapsulates critical information that makes scalable overlay networking possible. Its design allows for high levels of segmentation, supports dynamic routing over IP infrastructure, and integrates easily with existing hardware and software platforms. The simplicity and efficiency of the VXLAN header also contribute to its broad adoption in both enterprise and service provider environments. Network engineers and architects rely on this structure to build agile, tenant-aware, and resilient data center networks that can adapt to the demands of modern cloud-native applications.

As the networking industry continues to move toward more dynamic and programmable architectures, the importance of understanding protocols like VXLAN and their headers becomes even greater. The VXLAN header is not just a technical specification—it is a tool that enables the virtualization of the network layer in much the same way that hypervisors virtualize compute resources. Through encapsulation and logical segmentation, VXLAN empowers organizations to manage their networks with greater precision, agility, and scalability than ever before. Its header structure, though modest in size, carries the weight of a virtualized networking revolution.

VXLAN Control Plane Options

The control plane in a VXLAN deployment is a critical component that determines how information about endpoints, such as MAC and IP address mappings, is learned and distributed across the VXLAN fabric. In traditional Ethernet networks, the control plane is largely distributed and relies on mechanisms like MAC learning and ARP broadcasts. However, in a VXLAN overlay network, where Layer 2 segments are extended over a Layer 3 infrastructure, these traditional methods need to be re-evaluated and adapted to maintain scalability, performance, and simplicity. The control plane in VXLAN is responsible for establishing and maintaining communication between VXLAN Tunnel Endpoints (VTEPs), enabling them to learn where endpoints are located and how to forward traffic accordingly. Several control plane options are available for VXLAN deployments, each with its own strengths, trade-offs, and use cases.

The most basic control plane method used in VXLAN is the flood-and-learn mechanism. This approach mirrors the behavior of traditional Ethernet by flooding unknown unicast, broadcast, and multicast traffic across the VXLAN overlay. VTEPs learn MAC addresses by inspecting the source address of incoming packets and storing the association between the MAC address and the source VTEP. This method is simple to implement and does not require integration with external routing protocols or controllers. It uses IP multicast to flood traffic to all interested VTEPs within a particular VXLAN segment. Each VTEP joins the appropriate multicast group based on the VXLAN Network Identifier (VNI), and traffic is sent to the group whenever the destination MAC is unknown.

While flood-and-learn is easy to deploy, it does not scale well in large environments. Relying on multicast creates additional overhead on the underlay network and increases complexity in managing multicast groups. Moreover, the flooding of broadcast and unknown unicast traffic can lead to performance degradation, especially in networks with a high number of VXLAN segments or endpoints. The lack of deterministic MAC learning and the dependence on data-plane learning make it difficult to achieve fast convergence and efficient resource utilization. For these reasons, flood-and-learn is often seen as a starting point for small-scale or proof-of-concept deployments but is less suitable for production-grade data centers.

To address the limitations of flood-and-learn, the industry developed control plane alternatives that provide greater scalability, efficiency, and control. One of the most widely adopted control plane solutions for VXLAN is BGP EVPN, or Border Gateway Protocol Ethernet Virtual Private Network. BGP EVPN transforms the way VXLAN networks operate by introducing a control plane protocol that distributes Layer 2 and Layer 3 reachability information among VTEPs using the BGP routing protocol. With EVPN, VTEPs no longer rely on flooding to discover endpoint locations. Instead, they exchange MAC and IP address mappings through BGP updates, creating a more deterministic and scalable learning process.

BGP EVPN operates by advertising several types of routes that carry endpoint information. These include MAC route advertisements for Layer 2 reachability and IP prefix routes for Layer 3 reachability. Each route includes attributes such as the VNI, the next-hop IP address of the advertising VTEP, and optionally, the associated IP address of the endpoint. These advertisements allow all participating VTEPs to build a comprehensive and consistent view of the network, enabling them to forward traffic without flooding or unnecessary learning. The use of BGP as the underlying protocol also means that EVPN can be integrated into existing routing infrastructure, making it a natural choice for service providers and large enterprises.

The benefits of using EVPN as a VXLAN control plane are significant. It reduces the need for multicast in the underlay, thereby simplifying network design and improving performance. It enables faster convergence in response to topology changes, as updates are propagated through the control plane rather than relying on data-plane events. It also supports advanced features such as MAC mobility, which is essential in environments with workload migration and dynamic resource allocation. In addition, EVPN facilitates integrated routing and bridging, allowing VTEPs to perform both Layer 2 and Layer 3 forwarding in a consistent and scalable manner.

Another control plane option involves the use of centralized controllers, often found in software-defined networking architectures.

These controllers maintain a global view of the network and program forwarding tables on VTEPs based on policies, endpoint discovery, and intent-based logic. The controller approach provides strong consistency and simplifies management by centralizing the intelligence of the control plane. Controllers can dynamically allocate VNIs, manage tenant segmentation, and enforce security policies. They can also offer rich telemetry, analytics, and troubleshooting capabilities, which are difficult to achieve with distributed protocols alone.

However, the centralized controller model introduces its own challenges. It requires a reliable, scalable, and highly available control platform, as a failure in the controller infrastructure could impact the entire network. It also introduces a dependency on the controller's API and ecosystem, potentially limiting interoperability or requiring vendor lock-in. Despite these concerns, controller-based control planes are gaining popularity in environments where tight integration with cloud orchestration platforms and automated service delivery are essential.

Some deployments may choose to use static control plane configurations, where MAC-to-VTEP mappings are manually configured. This approach is extremely limited in scalability and flexibility but may be acceptable in small or highly deterministic environments. Static mappings eliminate the need for control plane protocols altogether but require careful planning and manual updates whenever changes occur. This method is rarely used in production and is generally reserved for test labs or highly isolated networks.

The choice of VXLAN control plane depends on several factors, including the size and scale of the network, the desired level of automation, the performance and convergence requirements, and the existing network architecture. Flood-and-learn offers simplicity but suffers in scale and efficiency. BGP EVPN provides a robust and scalable distributed control plane that integrates well with existing routing infrastructure. Controller-based approaches offer centralized intelligence and policy enforcement but require significant infrastructure and operational maturity.

VXLAN's flexibility in supporting multiple control plane options makes it adaptable to a wide range of deployment scenarios. Whether operated in a small enterprise with minimal infrastructure or in a large multi-tenant cloud data center with dynamic orchestration, the right control plane can ensure that the overlay network performs efficiently, remains scalable, and meets the evolving needs of modern applications. The control plane is not just about route distribution; it is the nervous system of the VXLAN architecture, responsible for ensuring that the overlay fabric is intelligent, responsive, and capable of supporting the demands of a software-defined world.

VXLAN with Multicast Flood and Learn

The initial implementation of VXLAN was designed to replicate traditional Ethernet behavior in virtualized data center environments by using a mechanism known as multicast flood and learn. This approach allowed VXLAN to maintain compatibility with legacy Layer 2 networking paradigms, which rely heavily on broadcast, unknown unicast, and multicast (BUM) traffic to operate. By extending these behaviors across a Layer 3 IP network through tunneling, multicast flood and learn made it possible for VXLAN to support features such as ARP requests, broadcast discovery protocols, and MAC address learning in virtual networks, thereby delivering Layer 2-like connectivity over an IP underlay.

In this model, VXLAN encapsulates Ethernet frames in UDP packets and uses IP multicast groups to disseminate BUM traffic across the overlay network. Each VXLAN segment, identified by its VXLAN Network Identifier (VNI), is associated with a specific multicast group. VXLAN Tunnel Endpoints, or VTEPs, join the appropriate multicast group for each VNI they are configured to participate in. When a VTEP receives a packet destined for an unknown MAC address, or when it needs to transmit a broadcast frame, it encapsulates the packet with a VXLAN header and sends it to the multicast group corresponding to the VNI. All other VTEPs subscribed to that group receive the packet, process it, and update their local MAC address tables based on the source information in the frame.

This flood and learn behavior mirrors what happens in traditional Ethernet switches, where unknown unicast frames are flooded out all ports and MAC addresses are learned by observing the source address of incoming traffic. By recreating this behavior in an overlay network, multicast flood and learn allows VXLAN to function transparently with existing applications and services that expect standard Ethernet semantics. This includes protocols like DHCP, ARP, and various discovery mechanisms that rely on broadcast communication to function properly. As a result, this VXLAN deployment model facilitates seamless integration of legacy workloads into virtualized environments without requiring modifications to applications or host configurations.

The use of multicast in this context, however, introduces specific requirements on the underlay IP network. The infrastructure must support IP multicast routing and ensure that multicast packets are properly forwarded to all interested receivers. Protocols such as Protocol Independent Multicast (PIM) are typically deployed to manage multicast distribution trees and to allow routers to forward multicast traffic efficiently across the fabric. Each multicast group used by VXLAN must be properly mapped to its associated VNI, and VTEPs must signal their interest in joining these groups through Internet Group Management Protocol (IGMP) messages. These mechanisms must be consistently supported across the entire underlay, which increases operational complexity and places demands on hardware and configuration.

Despite its operational simplicity at the overlay level, multicast flood and learn scales poorly in large environments. The replication of BUM traffic to every VTEP in a multicast group results in a high volume of unnecessary traffic, particularly when the number of endpoints or the number of VXLAN segments increases. Each broadcast or unknown unicast frame must be transmitted to all members of the multicast group, regardless of whether the destination endpoint is present on that particular VTEP. This leads to inefficient use of bandwidth and processing resources, which can be especially problematic in high-density environments or in data centers that operate at large scale.

Furthermore, multicast routing protocols can be complex to implement and troubleshoot. Ensuring that multicast trees are correctly formed and that traffic reaches all intended recipients without loops or delays requires careful configuration and continuous monitoring. In some cases, multicast support may not be available or desirable in the underlay network, particularly in brownfield deployments where network infrastructure is shared with legacy systems. These constraints have led many organizations to consider alternative control plane mechanisms, such as BGP EVPN, which eliminates the need for multicast altogether.

Nevertheless, multicast flood and learn remains an important deployment option for VXLAN, especially in environments where simplicity and compatibility are primary concerns. It provides a functional starting point for network virtualization, enabling administrators to extend Layer 2 networks without requiring an overhaul of the existing architecture. This makes it appealing for proof-of-concept environments, lab testing, or smaller production networks that do not require the scalability or performance benefits of a control plane-driven approach. In such cases, multicast flood and learn offers a familiar operational model and can be implemented relatively quickly with minimal dependencies.

In addition to its core functions, VXLAN with multicast flood and learn can be enhanced through the use of hardware acceleration and optimized forwarding mechanisms. Many modern network devices support VXLAN offload, allowing encapsulation and decapsulation to be performed in hardware rather than in software. This reduces CPU overhead on hypervisors and improves overall network performance. Some platforms also support intelligent replication strategies, such as head-end replication, which can reduce multicast dependency by sending multiple unicast copies of a packet to VTEPs, thereby emulating multicast behavior without requiring full underlay multicast support.

Head-end replication is particularly useful in scenarios where multicast is not available or not fully supported. In this model, the originating VTEP replicates the packet for each remote VTEP in the same VNI and sends each copy as a unicast VXLAN packet. While this approach increases bandwidth usage on the originating VTEP, it avoids the complexities of multicast and enables VXLAN overlays to function on simpler IP underlays. Some vendors use a combination of multicast and head-end replication, depending on the topology and platform capabilities, to provide a hybrid solution that balances compatibility and scalability.

Security considerations also arise with the use of multicast flood and learn. Because BUM traffic is sent to all VTEPs within a multicast group, there is potential for information leakage if isolation is not properly enforced. Tenant traffic could be visible to unauthorized recipients if multicast groups are misconfigured or if VTEPs are improperly included in multicast group membership. This underscores the importance of strict configuration validation and adherence to segmentation policies when deploying VXLAN using this model.

VXLAN with multicast flood and learn remains a relevant and valid control plane option in certain scenarios, especially where simplicity and compatibility with traditional Ethernet behavior are desirable. While it may not offer the same level of efficiency and scalability as more advanced control plane solutions, it serves as an effective mechanism for bootstrapping virtual network overlays and supporting legacy workloads. For organizations beginning their journey into network virtualization, it provides an accessible entry point, enabling them to understand and evaluate VXLAN technology without significant initial investment or complexity. The evolution of VXLAN control planes may offer more sophisticated solutions, but multicast flood and learn continues to hold its place in the landscape of overlay networking.

VXLAN with EVPN Control Plane

The combination of VXLAN and EVPN represents a significant advancement in the evolution of network virtualization, offering a scalable, efficient, and dynamic overlay architecture that overcomes the limitations of traditional flood-and-learn mechanisms. Ethernet Virtual Private Network, or EVPN, serves as a modern control plane for VXLAN overlays, leveraging the Border Gateway Protocol (BGP) to distribute endpoint information between VXLAN Tunnel Endpoints (VTEPs). This approach introduces a level of determinism, control, and visibility that flood-based methods cannot match, enabling large-scale deployments that require fine-grained traffic management, tenant isolation, and seamless workload mobility.

EVPN transforms the VXLAN control plane from a reactive, data-plane learning model into a proactive, control-plane-driven architecture. In traditional VXLAN with multicast flood-and-learn, VTEPs discover MAC addresses by observing traffic flows and relying on broadcast and unknown unicast flooding. This results in unnecessary bandwidth consumption, suboptimal convergence times, and increased dependence on IP multicast in the underlay. By contrast, EVPN enables VTEPs to exchange MAC and IP address reachability information through BGP updates, creating a comprehensive, consistent, and synchronized view of the entire VXLAN overlay network. This model eliminates the need for BUM traffic flooding and enables optimized forwarding from the moment traffic flows begin.

EVPN uses multiple BGP route types to advertise information about endpoints. Route Type 2, known as MAC/IP Advertisement Route, is used to communicate MAC addresses and their associated IP addresses within a given VXLAN segment, along with the next-hop VTEP responsible for reaching that endpoint. This route includes attributes such as the VXLAN Network Identifier (VNI), Ethernet Segment Identifier (ESI), and Route Distinguisher (RD), allowing multiple tenants to use overlapping address spaces without conflict. These advertisements provide all participating VTEPs with the knowledge required to forward both Layer 2 and Layer 3 traffic without relying on learning through actual packet forwarding events. Route Type 3, or Inclusive Multicast Ethernet Tag Route, is used to signal VTEP membership in a given broadcast domain, enabling head-end replication or optimized multicast handling for BUM traffic if necessary.

The use of BGP as the transport mechanism for EVPN offers inherent scalability and interoperability. BGP was originally designed for use in large-scale routing environments, making it an ideal choice for disseminating endpoint reachability in multi-tenant data centers. It provides built-in support for route filtering, route reflection, and hierarchical architectures, which are essential in large deployments. In the context of EVPN, BGP sessions are established between VTEPs or between VTEPs and a route reflector, depending on the topology.

Route reflectors allow for a hub-and-spoke architecture where endpoint information is efficiently propagated throughout the VXLAN fabric without requiring full mesh peering between all VTEPs.

One of the key advantages of EVPN is its support for integrated Layer 2 and Layer 3 services within the same control plane. In VXLAN-EVPN deployments, VTEPs can be configured to act as distributed gateways, meaning they perform both bridging and routing functions for local endpoints. When a packet needs to be routed between subnets, the local VTEP handles the operation without sending the packet to a centralized gateway. This distributed gateway model improves performance by reducing latency and east-west traffic within the data center. It also simplifies network design, as each VTEP becomes a logical extension of the routing fabric, capable of enforcing policies and forwarding decisions at the edge.

EVPN also enables advanced features that are essential in modern cloud environments, such as MAC mobility. When a virtual machine or container moves from one host to another, the associated MAC and IP address are now reachable via a different VTEP. EVPN detects this change by receiving a new BGP update with the same MAC address but a different next-hop. It updates its control plane database and withdraws the previous route, ensuring that traffic is quickly redirected to the new location. This process occurs without flooding and results in minimal disruption to active connections, making it ideal for dynamic environments where workloads are frequently migrated or scaled.

Security and segmentation are also enhanced through the use of EVPN. Because the control plane explicitly signals which VTEPs are participating in each VNI and which MAC/IP addresses belong to which tenant, it becomes easier to enforce policies and prevent unauthorized traffic from entering the overlay. Each VNI can represent a different tenant or application, and route targets can be used to limit the distribution of BGP updates to only those peers that are authorized to participate in a given segment. This model ensures strong isolation between tenants and reduces the attack surface compared to flood-based VXLAN deployments.

Operational visibility is another area where EVPN shines. Because endpoint information is carried in BGP, network operators can use familiar routing tools to inspect the state of the overlay network. They can view route tables, next-hop relationships, and MAC/IP mappings directly through standard BGP commands. This simplifies troubleshooting and provides a deterministic framework for understanding how traffic will flow across the fabric. Telemetry and analytics platforms can also integrate with EVPN data to provide real-time insights into network performance, mobility events, and control plane stability.

EVPN-based VXLAN deployments are well suited for both greenfield and brownfield environments. In greenfield scenarios, network architects can design an entirely new fabric with EVPN as the native control plane, using modern leaf-spine topologies and distributed gateways. In brownfield environments, where existing VLANs and traditional Layer 2 constructs must be preserved, EVPN can be introduced incrementally to extend and virtualize those segments without disrupting current services. This flexibility makes EVPN a powerful tool for evolving the network infrastructure while maintaining compatibility with existing applications and operational models.

Automation is also deeply aligned with EVPN architecture. Because BGP EVPN lends itself to declarative configuration, it integrates naturally with network automation frameworks. Orchestration tools can dynamically provision VNIs, assign route targets, configure VTEPs, and manage policy enforcement across the VXLAN fabric. This programmability is essential in environments that rely on DevOps practices, agile application development, and rapid infrastructure scaling. It ensures that the network can respond to changing demands just as quickly as compute and storage resources.

VXLAN with EVPN control plane represents a paradigm shift in how data center and cloud networks are built and operated. By leveraging a proven routing protocol to distribute endpoint intelligence, EVPN brings precision, efficiency, and agility to overlay networking. It supports the demands of multi-tenancy, workload mobility, microsegmentation, and dynamic service delivery, all while simplifying operations and reducing reliance on legacy protocols. As network infrastructures become more virtualized, programmable, and distributed, the VXLAN-EVPN combination will continue to serve as a robust and future-ready foundation for scalable, intelligent, and high-performance data center networks.

VXLAN Deployment Models

VXLAN has become a widely adopted overlay technology for extending Layer 2 connectivity over Layer 3 networks, offering enhanced scalability, flexibility, and support for multi-tenancy. One of the reasons VXLAN is so versatile and attractive is the variety of deployment models it supports. These models can be tailored to fit different data center designs, organizational needs, and levels of infrastructure maturity. Depending on the desired level of control, scalability, performance, and complexity, VXLAN can be deployed in several distinct ways. These deployment models define how VXLAN Tunnel Endpoints, or VTEPs, are implemented and how the VXLAN fabric integrates with existing Layer 2 and Layer 3 infrastructure.

The simplest and most straightforward VXLAN deployment model involves implementing VTEPs at the hypervisor level. In this scenario, each hypervisor hosts a virtual switch capable of encapsulating and decapsulating VXLAN packets. The virtual switch, often a component of the virtualization platform, handles VXLAN functions entirely in software. This model is commonly used in virtualized data centers where the bulk of workloads are running on virtual machines. Because the VTEPs are integrated into the hypervisors, the VXLAN overlay is built directly between servers without requiring changes to the physical network infrastructure. This software-based approach is flexible, easy to deploy, and ideal for smaller environments or proof-of-concept deployments where high throughput is not the primary concern.

However, software-based VTEPs can introduce performance limitations due to CPU overhead. As the number of virtual machines and the volume of traffic increase, the hypervisors may become burdened with encapsulation and decapsulation tasks. To overcome this, many environments transition to hardware-based VXLAN deployments, where VTEPs are implemented on physical network switches. These switches are VXLAN-aware and can perform tunneling operations in hardware, significantly improving performance and scalability. Hardware VTEPs also enable the integration of bare-metal servers and physical appliances into the VXLAN fabric, which would otherwise be difficult to incorporate in a purely software-based overlay.

A popular hardware-based deployment model is the leaf-spine architecture, where the leaf switches act as VTEPs and the spine switches serve as a high-speed Layer 3 underlay. Each leaf switch connects to the spine layer and participates in VXLAN encapsulation for traffic entering or exiting the virtual network. This design supports equal-cost multi-path routing, providing consistent latency and bandwidth between any pair of endpoints. The use of hardware VTEPs also enables distributed gateway functionality, allowing each leaf switch to perform both bridging and routing for local workloads. This reduces the amount of traffic traversing the fabric and improves the efficiency of east-west communication within the data center.

In hybrid deployment models, VXLAN overlays are extended between software-based VTEPs on hypervisors and hardware-based VTEPs on physical switches. This approach provides the flexibility of supporting virtualized workloads alongside physical servers and legacy equipment. For example, a virtual machine on a hypervisor can communicate with a bare-metal database server over a VXLAN overlay, with the hardware switch acting as the intermediary VTEP. These hybrid deployments are common in enterprises that are transitioning to virtualization or adopting a phased approach to modernizing their data centers.

Another deployment model involves the use of centralized gateways or VXLAN routers. In this model, VTEPs provide bridging functionality within their respective VXLAN segments, but inter-VXLAN routing is handled by a centralized device. This gateway, often a core switch or dedicated router, performs routing between VXLAN segments and between VXLAN and non-VXLAN networks. While this centralized model simplifies policy enforcement and provides a single point of control, it can introduce latency and become a bottleneck in large environments. As a result, this model is more suitable for smaller deployments or use cases where centralized control is preferred over distributed performance.

As organizations embrace multi-site and hybrid cloud architectures, VXLAN deployment models have evolved to support data center interconnects. In these scenarios, VXLAN overlays are extended across geographically dispersed sites, allowing virtual networks to span multiple data centers or cloud regions. This model requires VXLAN-aware edge devices capable of tunneling traffic across WAN links or through IPsec VPNs for secure transport. Multisite VXLAN deployments are typically paired with BGP EVPN control planes, which ensure that MAC and IP address information is accurately propagated across all sites. This enables seamless workload mobility and consistent network policies regardless of physical location.

VXLAN can also be integrated with container networking in modern cloud-native environments. Container orchestration platforms like Kubernetes can be configured to use VXLAN for pod-to-pod communication across nodes. In these deployments, VXLAN overlays connect container hosts, allowing for consistent IP addressing and service discovery without requiring complex routing. Network plugins and container networking interfaces implement VTEPs on each host, encapsulating container traffic in VXLAN tunnels and forwarding it to the appropriate destination. This deployment model supports microservices architectures and enables dynamic scaling while maintaining network isolation and performance.

Overlay-underlay integration is another critical aspect of VXLAN deployment. VXLAN relies on an underlay IP network to transport encapsulated packets between VTEPs. The underlay must be designed to support high availability, consistent latency, and sufficient bandwidth to carry VXLAN traffic efficiently. In many deployments, the underlay uses Interior Gateway Protocols such as OSPF or IS-IS to establish routing paths, and ECMP is used to distribute traffic across multiple links. The underlay must also accommodate VXLAN's additional packet overhead, which may require configuring jumbo frames on all links to prevent fragmentation and ensure optimal performance.

Security considerations also influence VXLAN deployment models. Some environments require encryption of VXLAN traffic, especially when traversing public networks or untrusted infrastructure. While VXLAN does not include native encryption, it can be combined with security protocols such as IPsec or MACsec to provide confidentiality and integrity. Secure VXLAN deployments may also incorporate access control policies, firewall rules, and segmentation to ensure that only authorized endpoints can join or communicate within a given VNI.

The deployment model selected for VXLAN directly impacts the network's performance, scalability, operational complexity, and integration with existing infrastructure. Whether leveraging hypervisor-based software VTEPs, high-performance hardware switches, hybrid combinations, centralized gateways, or multi-site interconnects, VXLAN provides a flexible foundation for building virtual networks. These deployment models support diverse use cases ranging from traditional enterprise applications to modern cloud-native workloads, enabling organizations to design their networks based on current needs while retaining the flexibility to evolve and scale over time.

VXLAN and Layer 2 Connectivity

VXLAN was designed to address the scalability and flexibility limitations of traditional Layer 2 networks, particularly in large-scale virtualized environments where the need for Layer 2 adjacency extends beyond the boundaries of a single physical location. At the heart of this capability is VXLAN's ability to encapsulate Ethernet frames and transport them over an IP network, effectively extending Layer 2 domains across a Layer 3 underlay. This functionality enables seamless connectivity between workloads regardless of their physical placement in the data center, allowing virtual machines, containers, or even physical devices to communicate as though they were part of the same broadcast domain.

Traditional Ethernet networks rely on switches to forward frames based on MAC address tables, with all devices within the same VLAN belonging to a single broadcast domain. This model works well in small environments but becomes inefficient and difficult to scale in large networks due to constraints such as the 4096 VLAN limit and the inefficiency of flooding mechanisms for unknown unicast, broadcast, and multicast traffic. Moreover, Layer 2 domains in traditional networks are generally constrained to a single Layer 2 boundary, meaning that extending these domains across data centers or between racks requires complex configurations, such as VLAN trunking or proprietary tunneling protocols.

VXLAN solves these challenges by encapsulating Layer 2 Ethernet frames inside UDP packets that can traverse a Layer 3 infrastructure. Each virtual Layer 2 network in VXLAN is identified by a 24-bit VXLAN Network Identifier (VNI), which allows for over 16 million isolated segments, vastly expanding the number of available broadcast domains. This encapsulation enables the creation of logical Layer 2 networks that are independent of the physical network topology. When a device sends a frame to another device in the same VNI, the frame is encapsulated at the source VXLAN Tunnel Endpoint (VTEP) and transmitted across the IP network to the destination VTEP. At the receiving end, the VTEP decapsulates the packet and delivers the original Ethernet frame to the destination device.

Layer 2 connectivity in VXLAN is primarily provided by the VXLAN VTEPs, which function as virtual switches or routers. These VTEPs can be implemented in software within hypervisors or in hardware on physical switches. Regardless of implementation, the VTEP's role is to map locally attached MAC addresses to remote VTEPs using a control plane or learning mechanism, encapsulate outbound frames, and decapsulate inbound frames. This setup ensures that Layer 2 communication between endpoints in the same VNI is preserved, even if those endpoints reside on different hosts, racks, or data centers.

To maintain Layer 2 adjacency, VXLAN must support the basic features of Ethernet switching, including MAC address learning and support for broadcast and multicast traffic. In deployments that use flood-and-learn mechanisms, VTEPs learn MAC addresses by observing the source MAC address of incoming frames and associating it with the sender's IP address. Unknown destinations are handled by flooding the packet to all other VTEPs within the same VNI, typically using multicast. This process mimics the behavior of traditional Ethernet switches but can lead to scalability and performance issues as the number of VTEPs and broadcast domains grows.

To address the limitations of flood-based learning, modern VXLAN deployments increasingly use control plane protocols like BGP EVPN. EVPN allows VTEPs to exchange MAC address mappings using BGP, providing a more scalable and deterministic method of maintaining Layer 2 connectivity. Instead of flooding, each VTEP is pre-informed of the location of every MAC address in the network, which greatly reduces broadcast traffic and accelerates convergence. This control plane-driven model also supports advanced features such as MAC mobility, allowing endpoints to move between VTEPs without disrupting connectivity or requiring relearning of MAC address locations.

One of the critical benefits of VXLAN's Layer 2 connectivity is workload mobility. Virtual machines can migrate from one hypervisor to another without changing their IP or MAC addresses. The VXLAN overlay ensures that their network identity and reachability are maintained throughout the move. This feature is essential for high availability, disaster recovery, and resource optimization in virtualized environments. It also supports live migration capabilities, such as VMware vMotion, by maintaining continuous Layer 2 connectivity during the migration process.

In addition to virtualized environments, VXLAN Layer 2 connectivity can be extended to include bare-metal servers and physical devices. This is achieved through hardware VTEPs on physical switches, which bridge physical ports to VXLAN segments. As a result, non-virtualized workloads, including appliances, storage systems, or legacy applications, can participate in VXLAN overlays and communicate with virtual workloads without any changes to their configuration. This ability to unify virtual and physical domains within a single overlay network simplifies operations and extends the benefits of network virtualization across the entire data center.

VXLAN Layer 2 connectivity also plays a significant role in multi-tenant architectures. Each tenant can be assigned a unique VNI, providing complete isolation between broadcast domains. This approach ensures that traffic from one tenant cannot reach another tenant's network, even if both operate on the same physical infrastructure. It also enables overlapping IP or MAC addresses, as each VNI maintains its own isolated MAC address space. This level of isolation is critical for service providers and large enterprises that host multiple customers or business units on shared infrastructure.

For applications that rely heavily on Layer 2 services, such as clustering protocols, broadcast-based discovery, or legacy systems, VXLAN provides the necessary framework to ensure compatibility. By supporting broadcast and multicast traffic within a VNI, VXLAN allows these applications to function without modification. Some implementations also include mechanisms for IGMP snooping and multicast optimization to reduce unnecessary flooding and improve efficiency in networks where multicast is used.

Network administrators must also consider MTU sizing when deploying VXLAN for Layer 2 connectivity. The encapsulation overhead introduced by VXLAN headers increases the total size of each frame. If the underlying network does not support sufficient MTU size, packets may be fragmented or dropped, leading to performance degradation. Therefore, configuring jumbo frames throughout the underlay network is a common best practice to ensure reliable transmission of encapsulated Layer 2 frames.

VXLAN's support for Layer 2 connectivity over Layer 3 networks represents a foundational shift in network architecture. It allows data center operators to design networks that are flexible, scalable, and aligned with modern application needs. The decoupling of logical Layer 2 domains from physical topologies enables a new level of agility in managing and deploying services. Whether in support of virtualization, multi-tenancy, hybrid cloud integration, or workload mobility, VXLAN provides the robust and adaptable Layer 2 connectivity needed to support the next generation of network infrastructure.

VXLAN and Layer 3 Connectivity

VXLAN was originally designed to extend Layer 2 segments across Layer 3 boundaries, providing virtualized Layer 2 connectivity between workloads distributed across physical networks. However, the scope of VXLAN is not limited to Layer 2. As data center architectures continue to evolve, Layer 3 connectivity within and across VXLAN overlays has become increasingly important. Modern applications often require communication across different subnets, and to accommodate this, VXLAN must provide efficient Layer 3 forwarding mechanisms while maintaining the benefits of virtual network abstraction. The integration of Layer 3 routing capabilities into VXLAN fabrics allows networks to support distributed services, multi-tier applications, and multi-tenant designs in a scalable and efficient manner.

Traditional data center designs often relied on centralized routing, where traffic between different subnets would be sent to a central router for inter-VLAN communication. This model, although simple, introduced inefficiencies in environments where most of the traffic flows were east-west, that is, between workloads within the data center. Sending every inter-subnet packet through a centralized gateway added latency, created bottlenecks, and increased the load on core routing devices. In VXLAN deployments, particularly those with EVPN control planes, the ability to perform distributed Layer 3 routing directly at the network edge represents a significant improvement over these legacy designs.

VXLAN with EVPN supports what is known as distributed anycast gateways. In this model, each VXLAN Tunnel Endpoint, typically located at the leaf switch or hypervisor level, acts as a default gateway for the locally attached workloads. These VTEPs share the same IP address and MAC address for the default gateway, enabling them to provide local routing services without requiring traffic to be forwarded to a centralized device. When a virtual machine or container sends a packet to a different subnet, the local VTEP performs the routing operation and forwards the packet over the VXLAN overlay to the destination VTEP. This approach minimizes latency, reduces congestion, and improves the overall efficiency of the network by keeping traffic as local as possible.

The distributed routing capability in VXLAN is enabled by the EVPN control plane, which advertises both MAC and IP address information across the VXLAN fabric. Through BGP updates, each VTEP learns the IP-to-MAC mappings and next-hop VTEPs for every endpoint in the overlay. When routing between subnets, the VTEP uses this information to encapsulate the routed packet into a VXLAN header and send it to the appropriate remote VTEP. The remote VTEP then decapsulates the packet and delivers it to the destination host. This process allows for seamless Layer 3 communication across the virtual network while preserving all the benefits of VXLAN encapsulation, including tenant isolation and segmentation.

Layer 3 connectivity in VXLAN is essential for multi-tenant environments where different tenants operate in different IP subnets. Each tenant may have multiple VNIs, representing separate Layer 2 segments, but often requires routing between them for application tiering or service integration. VXLAN with EVPN supports tenant-aware routing by using route targets to control the distribution of routing information. This allows only authorized VTEPs to receive and act upon routing updates for a given tenant, ensuring strict traffic isolation and policy enforcement. It also enables overlapping IP address spaces, where different tenants can use the same subnet ranges without conflict, because the VNI provides the necessary context to distinguish between them.

In addition to supporting intra-tenant routing, VXLAN and Layer 3 connectivity are critical for integrating the overlay network with external networks. In many deployments, services such as the internet, external VPNs, or legacy infrastructure reside outside the VXLAN fabric and require connectivity with workloads inside it. Border leaf switches or designated gateway devices are used to connect the VXLAN overlay with the traditional routing domain. These devices perform VXLAN-to-IP gateway functions, decapsulating VXLAN packets and routing them to external destinations, or vice versa. This boundary function must preserve network policies, perform necessary translations, and ensure consistent security enforcement across the overlay and underlay.

Another aspect of Layer 3 in VXLAN is the support for inter-site connectivity. As organizations expand to multiple data centers or hybrid cloud models, the ability to route between VXLAN overlays in different locations becomes crucial. With a properly designed underlay network and an EVPN control plane extended across sites, it is possible to build a unified Layer 3 overlay that spans geographic distances. Each site can maintain local VTEPs and distributed gateways while sharing IP and MAC information through BGP EVPN, enabling seamless routing between workloads regardless of their physical location. This architecture supports disaster recovery, load balancing, and application redundancy across sites, all while maintaining consistent IP addressing and routing behavior.

Security plays a significant role in Layer 3 VXLAN deployments. Because routing introduces the potential for traffic between different network segments, it is essential to enforce access control policies at routing boundaries. In distributed gateway scenarios, access control lists (ACLs), security groups, or firewall rules are applied at the VTEPs to restrict traffic according to tenant, subnet, or application-specific policies. These security mechanisms ensure that only authorized traffic is routed between subnets or to external networks. VXLAN deployments can also integrate with centralized policy controllers or SDN platforms that dynamically push policies to VTEPs based on identity, context, or application requirements.

Performance optimization is another key consideration when implementing Layer 3 connectivity in VXLAN. Because routing occurs at the VTEP, the underlying hardware or hypervisor must be capable of handling high throughput without introducing significant latency. In high-performance environments, hardware-based VTEPs on leaf switches offer line-rate routing with VXLAN encapsulation and decapsulation handled in silicon. This capability ensures that even with the additional overhead of routing and tunneling, the network can sustain large volumes of traffic without degradation. For environments relying on software VTEPs, offload capabilities in NICs and CPUs can help mitigate performance concerns.

Operational visibility into Layer 3 VXLAN traffic is critical for troubleshooting and maintaining network health. Tools that can correlate VXLAN encapsulated traffic with routing events, control plane changes, and underlay network conditions provide valuable insight. Monitoring Layer 3 paths, tracking route advertisements, and analyzing flow records help administrators ensure that VXLAN overlays are functioning as expected. These tools must understand both the overlay and underlay topologies, enabling a holistic view of traffic flows and potential bottlenecks.

The combination of VXLAN with Layer 3 connectivity delivers a highly scalable, efficient, and flexible networking model suitable for modern data centers and cloud environments. By integrating distributed routing directly into the overlay fabric, VXLAN ensures optimal traffic flow, seamless workload mobility, and secure tenant isolation. As applications continue to evolve and span multiple locations and services, VXLAN's ability to provide robust Layer 3 connectivity will remain a foundational capability for agile, resilient, and high-performance network infrastructures.

VXLAN in Multi-Tenant Environments

Multi-tenant environments have become a fundamental design principle in modern data centers, especially in cloud and service provider architectures where infrastructure is shared among multiple customers or business units. Each tenant requires secure, isolated networking resources to ensure privacy, compliance, and operational independence. As the demand for tenant isolation and network scalability has grown, traditional VLAN-based segmentation approaches have proven insufficient. VXLAN offers a robust and scalable alternative that provides logically isolated Layer 2 and Layer 3 segments across shared physical infrastructure. By enabling virtual networks that are abstracted from the underlying hardware, VXLAN empowers operators to build efficient, secure, and dynamic multi-tenant architectures.

At the heart of VXLAN's multi-tenancy capabilities is the VXLAN Network Identifier, or VNI. This 24-bit field, embedded in the VXLAN header, allows for more than 16 million unique segments, each acting as an independent virtual Layer 2 domain. In a multi-tenant environment, each tenant is assigned one or more VNIs, enabling the creation of isolated virtual networks that cannot communicate with each other unless explicitly permitted. This isolation ensures that traffic from one tenant does not interfere with or leak into another tenant's environment, addressing a fundamental requirement for secure multi-tenancy.

In traditional Ethernet networks, segmentation was typically achieved using VLANs. However, VLANs are limited to 4096 unique identifiers, which poses a significant scalability problem in environments hosting hundreds or thousands of tenants. VXLAN overcomes this limitation by supporting a vastly larger number of virtual segments. This allows operators to allocate unique VNIs to each tenant and even to each application tier within a tenant's environment, enabling fine-grained control and segmentation. Moreover, VNIs are not bound to the physical topology, allowing virtual networks to span across data centers and geographies without dependency on the constraints of Layer 2.

The VXLAN Tunnel Endpoints, or VTEPs, are the key components responsible for encapsulating and decapsulating traffic between VNIs. In a multi-tenant deployment, each VTEP is aware of the VNIs it serves and maintains MAC address mappings for endpoints within each tenant's virtual network. When a packet from a virtual machine or container is sent, the VTEP encapsulates the packet using the appropriate VNI and sends it to the destination VTEP. The destination VTEP then decapsulates the packet and delivers it to the endpoint within the corresponding tenant's virtual network. This process ensures that tenant traffic remains isolated throughout its journey across the shared infrastructure.

VXLAN supports both Layer 2 and Layer 3 isolation in multi-tenant designs. Layer 2 isolation is achieved through the VNI mechanism itself, which defines distinct broadcast domains. Layer 3 isolation, on the other hand, is provided by assigning separate IP subnets to each tenant and using distributed routing or centralized gateway devices that enforce routing policies. In VXLAN-EVPN deployments, BGP EVPN control plane extensions carry tenant-specific routing information, enabling efficient and policy-driven inter-VNI communication. Route targets and route distinguishers are used to identify and segregate tenant routes, ensuring that routing information is only shared with authorized VTEPs.

Security is paramount in multi-tenant environments, and VXLAN provides several mechanisms to enforce strong isolation and control. Each tenant's traffic is confined to its assigned VNI, which acts as a secure boundary. Additionally, access control lists, security groups, and firewall policies can be applied at VTEPs to further restrict communication based on source or destination IP, protocol, or port. This capability enables micro-segmentation within each tenant's environment, allowing for granular policy enforcement between application tiers or workloads. In some architectures, tenants may be granted control over their own virtual firewalls or routers, providing them with autonomy while maintaining centralized visibility and governance.

Another benefit of VXLAN in multi-tenant environments is the support for overlapping IP address spaces. Since each VNI represents an isolated virtual network, different tenants can use identical IP ranges without conflict. This flexibility simplifies migration scenarios, allows for easier onboarding of tenants, and reduces the burden of global IP address management. The combination of VNI-based segmentation and EVPN route control ensures that overlapping addresses are kept separate and that traffic is correctly forwarded based on the tenant context.

Scalability is a critical consideration in multi-tenant networks. VXLAN's architecture is inherently designed to scale horizontally. As more tenants are added, additional VNIs can be allocated without requiring significant changes to the physical infrastructure. VTEPs can be added dynamically, and with a control-plane-driven approach like EVPN, endpoint learning and route distribution remain efficient even as the number of tenants and endpoints grows. VXLAN overlays are also compatible with automation and orchestration tools, allowing for dynamic provisioning of tenant networks through APIs, infrastructure-as-code frameworks, and cloud management platforms.

In cloud service provider environments, VXLAN is frequently integrated with tenant self-service portals and orchestration platforms, allowing tenants to create and manage their own networks within predefined constraints. This automation reduces the operational burden on administrators and speeds up service delivery. Network abstraction through VXLAN also enables multi-tenancy in containerized environments, where Kubernetes or other orchestration tools may assign tenant workloads to shared hosts. VXLAN can provide the necessary isolation between tenants at the network level, regardless of how densely workloads are packed onto physical resources.

Multi-site and hybrid cloud deployments benefit significantly from VXLAN's multi-tenant capabilities. VXLAN overlays can be extended across wide area networks, enabling tenants to maintain consistent network policies and connectivity between on-premises and cloud environments. EVPN-based VXLAN designs support MAC mobility and cross-site routing, allowing tenant workloads to move freely without losing network context or violating isolation boundaries. This capability supports disaster recovery, load balancing, and flexible application scaling across geographic locations.

Operational visibility and troubleshooting in multi-tenant VXLAN environments require enhanced monitoring tools that understand both the overlay and underlay. Telemetry data, flow analysis, and endpoint tracking must all be tenant-aware to provide actionable insights. Network administrators need tools that can correlate VNIs with tenant identities, monitor tunnel health, and detect anomalies without breaching tenant privacy. Integration with logging, SIEM, and analytics platforms is essential for maintaining security and performance in a multi-tenant context.

VXLAN in multi-tenant environments provides the foundational infrastructure for building modern, scalable, and secure virtual networks. It empowers organizations to efficiently deliver networking services to multiple tenants while maintaining strict isolation and compliance. Whether deployed in enterprise data centers, public clouds, or hybrid architectures, VXLAN's support for massive segmentation, policy-driven routing, and dynamic provisioning makes it the overlay technology of choice for multi-tenant designs. Its compatibility with both traditional and cloud-native architectures ensures it can meet the diverse needs of tenants while simplifying network operations for providers.

VXLAN Troubleshooting and Tools

Troubleshooting VXLAN networks can be considerably more complex than traditional Ethernet or IP-based networks due to the added abstraction layers introduced by overlays. While VXLAN offers significant scalability, isolation, and flexibility, it also introduces new points of failure, increased dependency on tunneling, and a blend of overlay and underlay communication paths that must function in harmony. Network engineers tasked with maintaining VXLAN environments must be familiar with a broad set of tools and methodologies capable of inspecting traffic that has been encapsulated, identifying tunnel behavior, and understanding how the control plane and data plane interact within the VXLAN framework.

One of the key challenges in VXLAN troubleshooting is visibility. In traditional Layer 2 or Layer 3 networks, packet flows can be monitored and analyzed with standard tools such as ping, traceroute, and packet captures on physical interfaces. In VXLAN, however, packets are encapsulated within UDP datagrams, and the original Ethernet frame becomes the payload of a new packet. This means traditional tools may not provide insight into what is happening inside the tunnel unless they are VXLAN-aware or capable of decoding the encapsulated traffic. Understanding this encapsulation process is critical. A frame from a virtual machine is wrapped with a VXLAN header, UDP header, IP header, and Ethernet header before being transmitted across the underlay. Each layer of this stack must be inspected to fully understand the traffic path and identify where problems may be occurring.

To troubleshoot VXLAN networks effectively, it is necessary to analyze both the overlay and underlay. The overlay represents the logical VXLAN segments, VNI identifiers, and encapsulated traffic between virtual endpoints. The underlay is the physical IP network that carries the VXLAN-encapsulated packets. A failure in either layer can result in packet loss, degraded performance, or complete communication failure. For example, if two VTEPs are unable to reach each other over the underlay due to a routing issue, the overlay will not function, even if the configuration at the VXLAN level is correct. Tools that can validate IP connectivity between VTEPs, such as ICMP-based tests or UDP port probes, help confirm underlay health.

VXLAN connectivity begins with proper VTEP configuration. If VTEPs are misconfigured or cannot resolve each other's IP addresses, tunnels will not form correctly. It is essential to confirm that each VTEP has the appropriate VXLAN interface, correct source IP, and mapping of VNIs to tenant networks. Command-line interface (CLI) tools available on most switches and hypervisors allow engineers to verify the status of VTEPs, list known remote VTEPs, and display the mapping of MAC addresses to tunnel endpoints. In EVPN-based VXLAN deployments, additional troubleshooting commands are available to inspect BGP neighbors, route advertisements, and MAC/IP entries received through the control plane.

Packet capture remains one of the most powerful troubleshooting tools in a VXLAN environment. Capturing traffic at both the virtual switch level and the physical interface provides insight into the encapsulation and decapsulation processes. At the source, a packet should be seen entering the virtual switch, being encapsulated with a VXLAN header, and exiting the VTEP toward the underlay. On the receiving side, the encapsulated packet should arrive at the destination VTEP, be decapsulated, and be delivered to the intended virtual interface. Any deviation from this expected behavior, such as missing encapsulation, incorrect VNI values, or mismatched MAC addresses, can be quickly identified with packet inspection tools like Wireshark or tcpdump, provided those tools are configured to decode VXLAN headers.

In environments that use multicast for flood-and-learn behavior, it is critical to verify multicast group membership and IGMP configuration. Multicast troubleshooting involves checking that VTEPs are correctly joining multicast groups and that multicast routing is operational in the underlay network. Misconfigured or missing multicast group memberships can result in broadcast traffic being dropped, leading to incomplete MAC learning or failed ARP resolution. Tools that inspect IGMP group membership, as well as those that monitor multicast tree formation, help validate this aspect of the VXLAN deployment.

In control-plane-based VXLAN designs that use EVPN, troubleshooting expands to include BGP neighbor relationships and route propagation. Engineers must verify that BGP sessions are established between all relevant peers and that EVPN route types, such as MAC/IP advertisements and inclusive multicast routes, are being exchanged properly. Tools built into network operating systems can display received and advertised EVPN routes, their associated VNIs, and the MAC and IP bindings they contain. A failure to receive expected routes often indicates a problem with BGP policy, route targets, or EVPN configuration inconsistencies.

For visibility into VXLAN tunnel performance, telemetry tools are becoming increasingly valuable. Modern network fabrics support telemetry protocols such as sFlow, NetFlow, and IPFIX, which can provide flow-level visibility into VXLAN traffic. These protocols can be extended to include tunnel identifiers, such as the VNI, allowing for tenant-aware traffic analysis. Real-time monitoring platforms collect this data and present dashboards that show traffic rates, top talkers, dropped packets, and tunnel health. These insights help pinpoint issues such as congestion, asymmetric routing, or misrouted flows that might not be obvious from static configuration checks.

Troubleshooting VXLAN also involves ensuring that the physical infrastructure supports features required for VXLAN operation. The underlay network must be capable of handling larger MTU sizes due to VXLAN encapsulation overhead. Failure to accommodate jumbo frames can result in packet fragmentation or drops, especially for traffic that approaches the traditional 1500-byte MTU. Path MTU discovery tools and interface-level MTU checks can confirm whether the network is appropriately configured. Additionally, hardware support for VXLAN offload must be validated to ensure that devices perform encapsulation and decapsulation at line rate.

Automation and validation tools are also emerging as essential components in VXLAN troubleshooting. Infrastructure-as-code platforms can verify network configuration consistency, ensuring that VTEPs are properly provisioned and synchronized. Automated configuration audits and compliance checks prevent drift and highlight misaligned settings across distributed switches. Intent-based networking tools can continuously monitor network state and alert operators when the actual state diverges from the desired configuration, enabling faster identification of root causes.

VXLAN troubleshooting requires a holistic understanding of both the overlay and underlay network layers, along with the control plane mechanisms that support encapsulated traffic. Effective use of monitoring, packet inspection, route validation, and telemetry tools is essential for maintaining the stability and performance of the VXLAN fabric. As VXLAN becomes a foundational technology in cloud and data center environments, the ability to troubleshoot it effectively is a critical skill for network engineers. The complexity of overlay networking demands precision, and successful operations depend on the visibility and insight that proper tools and methodology can provide.

Introduction to NVGRE

Network Virtualization using Generic Routing Encapsulation, or NVGRE, is one of the early technologies developed to address the growing need for scalable, isolated, and flexible virtual networking in modern data centers. As organizations began adopting virtualization at scale, the limitations of traditional networking mechanisms such as VLANs became increasingly apparent. With only 4096 VLAN IDs available, VLANs could not meet the demands of large-scale multi-tenant environments or complex cloud architectures. NVGRE was introduced as a solution to this problem by providing a way to encapsulate Layer 2 traffic within Layer 3 packets, enabling the creation of isolated virtual networks that can be transported over standard IP infrastructure.

NVGRE was proposed by Microsoft and its partners as a method to decouple the logical network from the physical network, allowing virtual machines and other workloads to be connected across disparate physical locations while maintaining the appearance of being on the same Ethernet segment. This was particularly important in environments using Microsoft's Hyper-V virtualization platform, where the need to support tenant isolation, workload mobility, and dynamic provisioning of virtual networks was rapidly growing. NVGRE aimed to offer a scalable, standards-based encapsulation technique that could integrate tightly with existing routing and switching hardware.

At its core, NVGRE uses the well-established GRE protocol to encapsulate Ethernet frames. GRE, or Generic Routing Encapsulation, is a tunneling protocol that allows various network layer protocols to be encapsulated within IP packets. In the context of NVGRE, GRE is used to wrap Layer 2 Ethernet frames so that they can be transported across an IP-based network. Each NVGRE packet consists of the original Ethernet frame, a GRE header, and an outer IP header. This encapsulated packet can then be routed like any other IP packet across the physical network, which is often referred to as the underlay. At the destination, the NVGRE endpoint decapsulates the packet and forwards the original Ethernet frame to the appropriate virtual machine or tenant network.

A critical component of the NVGRE header is the Tenant Network Identifier, or TNI. This 24-bit field is embedded in the GRE key field and functions similarly to the VXLAN Network Identifier in VXLAN. It uniquely identifies a tenant's virtual network, allowing multiple isolated networks to coexist on the same physical infrastructure. With 24 bits, NVGRE can support over 16 million unique tenant networks, solving the VLAN scalability issue and enabling large-scale multi-tenancy in service provider and enterprise environments. Each NVGRE endpoint uses the TNI to determine how to handle the incoming traffic and to maintain traffic separation between tenants.

NVGRE endpoints, also referred to as Network Virtualization Edge (NVE) components, are responsible for encapsulating and decapsulating packets. These endpoints can be implemented in software, such as within the Hyper-V virtual switch, or in hardware, such as in NVGRE-aware network adapters or physical switches. The NVE maintains mappings of virtual IP addresses, MAC addresses, and tenant identifiers, ensuring that traffic is correctly routed to the appropriate virtual network. These mappings can be populated through centralized control mechanisms, such as Microsoft's Network Virtualization Generic Routing Encapsulation Policy Server (NVGRE Policy Server), or through dynamic learning processes.

One of the key motivations behind NVGRE's development was the need for seamless integration with existing enterprise networking infrastructure. NVGRE leverages standard IP routing and GRE encapsulation, both of which are well understood and widely supported by networking hardware. This design decision allows NVGRE to function over any IP network without requiring significant changes to the existing underlay. It also supports Equal-Cost Multi-Path (ECMP) routing, enabling the use of multiple network paths to distribute traffic and improve performance and redundancy. By encapsulating traffic in IP packets, NVGRE allows for efficient use of network bandwidth and infrastructure resources.

NVGRE was designed with Hyper-V environments in mind, and its integration into the Microsoft ecosystem is one of its defining characteristics. In Microsoft's System Center and Windows Server platforms, NVGRE is used to support Virtual Machine Networks (VM Networks), providing each tenant or workload with a logically isolated network. This integration enables features such as dynamic network provisioning, workload mobility, and tenant self-service capabilities. NVGRE also supports the use of gateway devices that provide connectivity between NVGRE virtual networks and traditional physical networks or the Internet, enabling hybrid connectivity scenarios.

Despite its strengths, NVGRE has not achieved the same level of adoption as other overlay technologies like VXLAN. One of the reasons is its limited interoperability with non-Microsoft environments. While GRE is a standard protocol, the specific implementation of NVGRE and its reliance on Microsoft's management tools and policy servers make it less attractive in heterogeneous data center environments. Additionally, the lack of native support in many hardware switches and the absence of a control plane standard equivalent to EVPN for NVGRE have limited its scalability and operational efficiency in comparison to VXLAN-based solutions.

However, NVGRE remains a relevant technology in Microsoft-centric infrastructures, especially in private clouds and enterprise networks built on Hyper-V and System Center Virtual Machine Manager. Its design principles laid the groundwork for later technologies and helped to shape the evolution of network virtualization. The encapsulation model, use of tenant identifiers, and integration with existing routing infrastructure introduced by NVGRE influenced the development of subsequent protocols that aim to provide even greater flexibility and interoperability.

From a troubleshooting and monitoring perspective, NVGRE introduces challenges similar to those found in other overlay networks. Visibility into encapsulated traffic requires tools capable of decoding GRE headers and understanding tenant identifiers. Traditional network monitoring tools may not provide insight into the virtual network layer unless they are specifically designed to interpret NVGRE packets. As a result, operational teams must be equipped with tools that provide end-to-end visibility across both the overlay and underlay networks. This includes packet capture utilities, flow analysis platforms, and management consoles that can correlate virtual and physical network data.

NVGRE also highlights the importance of careful planning in overlay deployments. Network administrators must ensure that the underlay supports sufficient MTU to accommodate GRE encapsulation overhead. If MTU settings are not properly configured across the network, fragmentation or packet drops may occur, impacting application performance. Coordination between server teams and network engineers is essential to ensure consistent configuration and optimal operation of the NVGRE fabric.

As organizations continue to pursue software-defined networking and network virtualization, the principles introduced by NVGRE remain highly relevant. Even as newer protocols gain traction, the need to decouple network services from physical infrastructure, support scalable multi-tenancy, and enable dynamic provisioning continues to drive the adoption of overlay technologies. NVGRE represents an important step in this journey, offering a Microsoft-native approach to virtual networking that aligns with the broader goals of flexibility, isolation, and scalability in modern data center design.

NVGRE Architecture and Components

The architecture of NVGRE, or Network Virtualization using Generic Routing Encapsulation, is designed to support scalable, isolated, and flexible network virtualization within cloud and enterprise data centers. Its purpose is to overcome the limitations of traditional network segmentation technologies like VLANs by leveraging IP-based tunneling through GRE encapsulation. NVGRE creates a virtualized Layer 2 network on top of a Layer 3 physical infrastructure, allowing virtual machines and workloads to maintain consistent network configurations regardless of their physical location within the data center. The architectural model of NVGRE revolves around several key components that work together to encapsulate traffic, maintain network separation, and manage dynamic communication between virtualized endpoints.

At the center of NVGRE architecture are the virtual networks, each assigned a unique Tenant Network Identifier, or TNI. The TNI is a 24-bit value embedded in the GRE key field, which functions similarly to the VXLAN Network Identifier in VXLAN deployments. The TNI serves as the primary mechanism for logically isolating tenant networks. It ensures that packets belonging to one virtual network are not visible or accessible to endpoints in other virtual networks. This identifier provides support for over sixteen million individual virtual networks, making NVGRE highly scalable and well-suited to large multi-tenant environments such as public and private clouds.

To transport tenant traffic across the physical infrastructure, NVGRE uses encapsulation. This encapsulation process takes a standard Layer 2 Ethernet frame generated by a virtual machine or physical server and wraps it within a GRE header, followed by an IP header, and finally a Layer 2 Ethernet header used for transmission across the underlay. This layered encapsulation transforms the frame into a routable packet suitable for transmission through IP-based networks. At the destination, the encapsulated packet is decapsulated to reveal the original Ethernet frame, which is then delivered to the receiving virtual machine or endpoint.

The primary functional component responsible for this encapsulation and decapsulation is the Network Virtualization Edge, or NVE. The NVE acts as the NVGRE Tunnel Endpoint. It resides either in a virtual switch within a hypervisor such as Hyper-V or in a physical network device, such as a top-of-rack switch or a network interface card capable of NVGRE processing. The NVE is responsible for interpreting the TNI, performing tunneling operations, and forwarding traffic based on MAC and IP mappings. In software implementations, this role is commonly handled by the Hyper-V virtual switch, which integrates seamlessly with Microsoft's networking stack. In hardware implementations, the NVE can be offloaded to switch silicon or intelligent NICs to enhance performance and reduce CPU load on host systems.

A critical component of NVGRE architecture is the management plane, which is responsible for maintaining network state, distributing policies, and managing address mappings between virtual and physical networks. In Microsoft's implementation, this management plane is facilitated by components such as the Windows Server Hyper-V Network Virtualization Policy Server. This server stores and distributes policies that map customer addresses, which are used within tenant networks, to provider addresses, which are used in the physical underlay. These mappings allow for isolation between tenants and enable each tenant to use overlapping IP address spaces without conflict. The Policy Server coordinates with each NVE to ensure consistent address translation and enforcement of routing policies.

Another essential architectural element is the customer address and provider address model. In NVGRE, customer addresses (CA) are the IP addresses assigned to virtual machines within their isolated virtual networks. These addresses remain unchanged regardless of the virtual machine's location or migration status. Provider addresses (PA), on the other hand, are the IP addresses used by the NVGRE overlay to transport encapsulated packets across the physical infrastructure. These addresses belong to the physical hosts or NVEs participating in the NVGRE fabric. The mapping between CAs and PAs is maintained by the management plane and enforced by the NVEs. This separation of addressing domains allows virtual machines to move across the data center without requiring changes to their IP addresses or loss of connectivity.

NVGRE also includes the concept of gateways, which are responsible for bridging the virtualized NVGRE environment with external networks. These gateways perform routing between NVGRE tenant networks and traditional VLAN or IP networks, providing access to shared services, the internet, or other physical network segments. A gateway in the NVGRE architecture may be implemented as a virtual appliance, a physical router, or a network service embedded within a switch. It is responsible for decapsulating inbound traffic, performing any necessary network address translation, and forwarding packets to their destination. Similarly, it encapsulates outbound packets from external networks into NVGRE format and routes them to the appropriate NVE.

In large-scale NVGRE deployments, traffic optimization becomes important to reduce the overhead associated with encapsulation and to maintain network efficiency. NVGRE supports Equal-Cost Multi-Path routing (ECMP), which allows encapsulated packets to be balanced across multiple paths in the physical network. This capability improves bandwidth utilization and increases resilience by providing alternate routes in the event of link or node failure. ECMP relies on hashing algorithms to distribute traffic based on packet header fields, which include source and destination addresses as well as the protocol type. The GRE encapsulation includes sufficient entropy to allow effective load balancing across ECMP paths.

While NVGRE is often tightly integrated into Microsoft environments, it also aligns with broader network virtualization principles and can interoperate with other network components if proper tunneling and encapsulation standards are supported. However, its dependence on the GRE protocol, and specifically the use of the GRE key field to carry the TNI, requires hardware and software to recognize and process these fields correctly. Not all network devices support NVGRE natively, which can limit the flexibility of deploying mixed-vendor environments unless intermediary translation or gateway devices are employed.

From a security perspective, NVGRE provides isolation through encapsulation and TNI-based separation, but it can also be enhanced by implementing IPsec tunnels or other encryption methods between NVEs. This ensures that tenant traffic remains confidential, especially when traversing shared infrastructure or untrusted network paths. NVGRE's architecture allows for the insertion of additional security functions such as firewalls, intrusion detection systems, or logging mechanisms at various points in the overlay and underlay, depending on the required policy enforcement.

The NVGRE architecture emphasizes modularity, scalability, and tenant abstraction. By introducing a separation between logical and physical network topologies, it provides the agility needed to support cloud-era networking. Its core components—the Tenant Network Identifier, GRE encapsulation, NVEs, policy servers, gateways, and separation of customer and provider addressing—work in unison to deliver a framework that enables dynamic provisioning, workload mobility, and multi-tenancy in a consistent and manageable way. NVGRE's structure reflects a fundamental shift toward software-defined networking, where programmability and virtualization reshape how networks are built, maintained, and scaled in modern IT environments.

NVGRE Encapsulation Format

The NVGRE encapsulation format is at the core of how Network Virtualization using Generic Routing Encapsulation functions. It enables the creation of isolated virtual Layer 2 networks over a shared Layer 3 IP infrastructure by wrapping Ethernet frames inside GRE tunnels. The encapsulation structure used by NVGRE is based on the well-known Generic Routing Encapsulation protocol, which has long been used to transport diverse payload types over IP networks. In the case of NVGRE, GRE is extended to carry Ethernet frames along with metadata necessary to maintain tenant separation and enable scalable network virtualization. Understanding the encapsulation format is essential to grasp how NVGRE achieves its goals of multi-tenancy, mobility, and abstraction from the physical network topology.

The encapsulation process in NVGRE begins with a standard Ethernet frame generated by a virtual machine, which may include a Layer 2 header, payload, and frame check sequence. This original frame is not modified but instead becomes the payload of a new packet that is suitable for transmission across an IP-routed network. To enable this, NVGRE adds a GRE header and an outer IP header. This encapsulated packet is then transmitted from the source NVGRE endpoint, typically a virtual switch or network interface card, across the underlay network to the destination endpoint, which performs decapsulation and delivers the original frame to the receiving virtual machine.

The GRE header in NVGRE is where the key differentiation occurs. In standard GRE, the header includes various flags and optional fields, one of which is the Key field. NVGRE uses the GRE Key field to encode the Tenant Network Identifier. The TNI is a 24-bit value that uniquely identifies the virtual network to which the encapsulated packet belongs. This field is critical for maintaining tenant isolation, as it allows the destination NVGRE endpoint to determine which virtual network the packet should be delivered to. Although the GRE Key field is technically 32 bits in length, NVGRE reserves the upper 8 bits and uses the lower 24 bits for the TNI. This design allows for more than sixteen million isolated virtual networks, addressing the scalability issues inherent in VLAN-based segmentation.

The GRE header in NVGRE typically includes the standard fields such as the Flags field, which is set to indicate that the Key field is present. In binary, this is represented by setting the K bit in the Flags field. The Protocol Type field is another critical component, indicating that the encapsulated payload is an Ethernet frame. The standard Ethernet protocol type value of 0x6558 is used to signify this. This value informs the decapsulating endpoint that the payload should be processed as a complete Layer 2 Ethernet frame, not simply as an IP packet or other data structure.

Following the GRE header is the outer IP header, which provides the routing information required to move the packet across the physical underlay network. The source and destination IP addresses in this header correspond to the IP addresses of the source and destination NVGRE endpoints. These are typically assigned from the provider address space and are unrelated to the tenant IP addresses carried within the encapsulated frame. The outer IP header allows the encapsulated packet to be routed just like any other IP packet, enabling full use of the underlay's routing and load balancing capabilities, including Equal-Cost Multi-Path routing. This is essential in modern data centers, where performance and fault tolerance depend on efficient use of available network paths.

At the transport layer, NVGRE does not rely on TCP or UDP. Instead, GRE is encapsulated directly over IP, meaning that the protocol field in the outer IP header is set to 47, which denotes GRE. This direct encapsulation reduces overhead compared to other tunneling methods that use UDP, such as VXLAN, because there is no need for transport layer port numbers or checksums. However, it also means that GRE-based tunnels like NVGRE are not inherently compatible with devices that perform deep packet inspection based on transport-layer information, and they may require special handling in some firewall or NAT configurations.

Once the encapsulated packet arrives at the destination NVGRE endpoint, the decapsulation process begins. The endpoint examines the outer IP header to verify the packet's validity and extracts the GRE header. From the GRE Key field, it retrieves the TNI, which is used to determine the appropriate virtual network context for the payload. The original Ethernet frame is then extracted and forwarded through the virtual switch or NIC to the destination virtual machine. If the TNI does not match any known virtual network on the endpoint, the packet is dropped to prevent misdelivery and ensure strict tenant isolation.

In addition to the TNI, NVGRE implementations maintain a mapping of virtual MAC and IP addresses to physical provider addresses. These mappings are often managed by a policy server or controller, which distributes this information to each NVGRE endpoint. The mapping ensures that traffic can be properly routed across the overlay by allowing the source endpoint to determine the correct destination provider address for a given virtual machine. This model supports overlapping IP addresses between tenants, since the overlay context defined by the TNI allows each tenant to maintain its own isolated address space.

Because NVGRE does not use a control plane protocol like EVPN, endpoint discovery and mapping distribution typically rely on a centralized management system or are statically configured. This can limit scalability and agility in large environments compared to protocols that support distributed learning and dynamic control plane operations. However, in tightly integrated Microsoft environments, this centralized management is facilitated by tools such as System Center Virtual Machine Manager, which can automate the provisioning of NVGRE networks and distribute policies to endpoints.

The encapsulation format used by NVGRE introduces additional bytes of overhead to each packet, which must be accounted for when configuring the underlay network. The added size from the GRE and IP headers increases the maximum transmission unit, or MTU, of the encapsulated packet. Network operators must ensure that all devices in the underlay path support jumbo frames or are configured with MTUs large enough to handle the increased packet size. Failure to do so can result in packet fragmentation or drops, negatively impacting performance and reliability.

NVGRE's encapsulation format represents a precise and structured method for supporting virtual networking at scale. By leveraging the GRE protocol and enhancing it with tenant-aware identifiers, NVGRE provides a mechanism for building isolated, scalable virtual networks on top of existing IP infrastructure. The encapsulation format defines the way traffic is abstracted from the physical network, enabling mobility, segmentation, and centralized policy enforcement. Although newer protocols have emerged, NVGRE's encapsulation approach continues to demonstrate the power of standardized tunneling mechanisms in supporting network virtualization across diverse and dynamic environments.

NVGRE and Microsoft Hyper-V Integration

NVGRE was developed with deep integration into Microsoft Hyper-V environments, making it a natural choice for enterprises and service providers leveraging Microsoft's virtualization technologies. As organizations began to virtualize their workloads at scale using Hyper-V, the limitations of VLAN-based network segmentation became a growing concern. VLANs, restricted to 4096 identifiers, were inadequate for the scalability needs of large, multi-tenant infrastructures. Microsoft addressed this issue by supporting NVGRE as a native network virtualization technology in Hyper-V, beginning with Windows Server 2012 and extending through subsequent versions. The result was a tightly coupled solution where NVGRE became a foundational element of Microsoft's Software Defined Networking (SDN) strategy.

In a Hyper-V environment, NVGRE works by encapsulating tenant traffic within GRE tunnels, allowing multiple isolated virtual networks to operate over the same physical infrastructure. Each virtual machine can retain its own IP address and network identity even as it moves between Hyper-V hosts. This is essential for enabling workload mobility, simplified management, and seamless communication across a dynamic data center environment. The encapsulation is handled directly by the Hyper-V virtual switch, which acts as a Network Virtualization Edge and performs GRE encapsulation and decapsulation without the need for external appliances or complex configurations.

At the heart of NVGRE's integration with Hyper-V is the concept of virtual networks, which are created and managed using System Center Virtual Machine Manager (SCVMM) or Windows PowerShell. A virtual network in Hyper-V with NVGRE support is associated with one or more Virtual Subnets, each mapped to a Tenant Network Identifier. This TNI, a 24-bit identifier embedded in the GRE key field, ensures that traffic is logically separated between tenants. The TNI enables each tenant to maintain its own isolated address space, including overlapping IP address ranges, without interference from other tenants operating in the same data center. This isolation is enforced by the Hyper-V virtual switch, which tags outbound packets with the appropriate TNI and filters inbound traffic accordingly.

One of the strengths of NVGRE in Hyper-V is its seamless integration with Microsoft's management and orchestration tools. SCVMM acts as the central policy and provisioning engine, allowing administrators to create virtual networks, assign IP address pools, and define routing policies from a single interface. It communicates with all participating Hyper-V hosts to ensure that each node receives consistent configuration and has the necessary mapping between customer and provider addresses. The provider address corresponds to the IP address assigned to the physical Hyper-V host, while the customer address is the virtual machine's IP within its isolated virtual subnet. This separation of addressing enables virtual machines to move freely without requiring changes to IP configurations or impacting connectivity.

Hyper-V hosts in an NVGRE deployment maintain a mapping table that associates each customer address with a provider address and a TNI. This table is dynamically populated through the policy server or SCVMM and used to determine how to encapsulate and route traffic. When a virtual machine sends a packet to another VM within the same virtual network but on a different host, the source Hyper-V host encapsulates the packet using the GRE format and forwards it to the destination Hyper-V host. The destination host decapsulates the packet and delivers it to the receiving VM. This process is transparent to the virtual machines, which believe they are communicating over a traditional Layer 2 network.

To enable communication between NVGRE networks and external resources, Microsoft provides the concept of gateway virtual machines or gateway appliances. These gateways route traffic between NVGRE virtual networks and physical networks, including the internet or other VLAN-based systems. Gateways perform network address translation and routing, ensuring that tenant traffic remains isolated while still allowing access to shared services such as domain controllers, databases, or public-facing applications. These gateway functions are deployed and managed via SCVMM, which also ensures high availability and load balancing as needed.

NVGRE in Hyper-V supports key enterprise networking features such as Quality of Service (QoS), security filtering, and access control lists, all of which can be enforced at the virtual switch level. These features allow administrators to apply tenant-specific policies and ensure compliance with internal and regulatory standards. Additionally, integration with Windows Firewall and Network Security Groups enhances security by allowing administrators to define granular traffic rules based on source and destination IPs, ports, and protocols. These rules can be dynamically adjusted through automation scripts or SCVMM templates, enabling responsive security management in cloud-scale environments.

Performance optimization is also addressed in Hyper-V with NVGRE support. GRE encapsulation introduces some additional overhead, which can impact CPU performance if handled entirely in software. To mitigate this, Microsoft introduced support for NVGRE offload in compatible network interface cards. With hardware offload, the encapsulation and decapsulation processes are performed directly on the NIC, freeing CPU resources and improving throughput. This hardware acceleration ensures that NVGRE networks can scale to meet the needs of high-bandwidth workloads such as database replication, backup traffic, or high-volume web services.

Troubleshooting NVGRE in Hyper-V environments is facilitated by a combination of Microsoft and third-party tools. Event logs, performance counters, and PowerShell diagnostics provide detailed insight into the operation of the virtual switch, GRE tunnels, and network policies. Administrators can use packet capture tools such as Microsoft Network Monitor or Wireshark, with appropriate GRE dissectors enabled, to observe encapsulated traffic and confirm the correct operation of tunneling, TNI tagging, and address translation. In larger deployments, integration with System Center Operations Manager or Azure Monitor provides real-time visibility into tunnel status, network health, and bandwidth usage, enabling proactive detection and resolution of potential issues.

The integration of NVGRE with Microsoft Hyper-V represents a complete and cohesive solution for network virtualization in Windows-based environments. It empowers administrators to create scalable, flexible, and secure virtual networks without being limited by physical infrastructure or traditional segmentation methods. Through deep integration with Microsoft's ecosystem of management tools, NVGRE enables automation, orchestration, and dynamic provisioning of virtual networks that support multi-tenancy, workload mobility, and hybrid cloud scenarios. This architecture allows organizations to deliver Infrastructure as a Service on their own terms while maintaining tight control over network configuration, security, and performance. The ability to abstract the network layer from the physical fabric and manage it entirely through software is one of the key benefits of NVGRE in Hyper-V, positioning it as a core enabler of Microsoft's broader vision for cloud computing and software-defined infrastructure.

NVGRE Scalability Considerations

As data centers continue to expand in both size and complexity, the need for scalable network virtualization solutions becomes more critical. NVGRE, or Network Virtualization using Generic Routing Encapsulation, was introduced to address the growing demand for network isolation and segmentation in large, multi-tenant environments. Designed with scalability in mind, NVGRE allows enterprises and service providers to create thousands or even millions of logically isolated virtual networks over a common physical infrastructure. However, achieving this level of scalability requires careful architectural planning, efficient control mechanisms, and a deep understanding of the protocol's operational constraints and capabilities.

One of the foundational scalability benefits of NVGRE lies in its use of the Tenant Network Identifier. Unlike traditional VLANs, which are limited to a 12-bit identifier and therefore support a maximum of 4096 segments, NVGRE uses a 24-bit TNI embedded in the GRE header. This expands the number of supported virtual networks to over sixteen million, making it possible to support a large number of tenants or application environments without exhausting identifier space. This massive segmentation capability is essential in service provider clouds, where each customer may require multiple isolated networks, or in enterprise environments that need to support highly segmented workloads for compliance, security, or operational reasons.

Beyond the numerical space provided by the TNI, scalability in NVGRE is also closely tied to how the overlay network interacts with the physical underlay. Since NVGRE encapsulates Layer 2 Ethernet frames in GRE and transmits them over IP networks, the performance and capacity of the underlay play a significant role in determining the overall scalability of the solution. The underlay must be designed to support high throughput, low latency, and fault tolerance. Equal-Cost Multi-Path routing is typically used to distribute traffic across multiple paths, allowing NVGRE to take advantage of link redundancy and parallelism in the physical network. Proper configuration of ECMP ensures that encapsulated traffic is balanced effectively, preventing congestion and maximizing bandwidth usage.

Another important scalability factor is the encapsulation overhead introduced by NVGRE. Each packet encapsulated with GRE carries additional headers, including the outer IP header and the GRE header itself. This increases the total packet size and can lead to fragmentation if the network does not support a sufficiently high Maximum Transmission Unit. In large environments, where performance and efficiency are paramount, all devices in the network must be configured to support jumbo frames that can accommodate the increased packet size. Failure to adjust MTU values appropriately across switches, routers, and NICs can lead to performance degradation, dropped packets, and unnecessary retransmissions.

Control plane management is another critical area that affects NVGRE scalability. Unlike protocols such as VXLAN with EVPN, NVGRE lacks a standardized distributed control plane. In most deployments, the mapping of tenant addresses to physical endpoints is managed by a centralized controller or policy server. This centralization simplifies management in smaller environments but can become a bottleneck as the number of tenants and endpoints grows. To scale effectively, the control infrastructure must be highly available, capable of fast updates, and optimized for large-scale state management. Efficient policy distribution mechanisms and synchronization across Hyper-V hosts or other NVGRE endpoints are essential to avoid stale data and ensure timely network convergence.

Hyper-V plays a significant role in NVGRE scalability, particularly in Microsoft-centric environments. Each Hyper-V host acts as a Network Virtualization Edge and maintains mappings between customer addresses and provider addresses. As more virtual machines are deployed, these mapping tables grow and require more memory and CPU resources to process and manage encapsulated traffic. In large-scale scenarios, performance tuning on Hyper-V hosts becomes necessary. This includes optimizing the virtual switch configuration, enabling offload capabilities on supported NICs, and ensuring that GRE encapsulation is handled by hardware wherever possible. Offloading GRE processing to the NIC reduces CPU overhead and allows the host to scale up the number of concurrently active virtual networks and virtual machines.

Gateways in NVGRE deployments also present scalability challenges. These gateways, whether virtual appliances or physical devices, are responsible for routing traffic between NVGRE overlays and external networks. In highly segmented environments, gateways must handle a high volume of encapsulated traffic, perform address translation, and enforce security policies. As more tenants or external connections are added, the demand on these gateways increases significantly. To ensure scalability, gateways must support load balancing, redundancy, and horizontal scaling. In some cases, multiple gateway instances may be deployed, each serving a subset of tenants, and managed centrally through System Center Virtual Machine Manager.

Operational tooling and monitoring must scale alongside the network itself. In NVGRE, the encapsulated nature of traffic makes it more challenging to gain visibility into packet flows and endpoint behavior. Standard monitoring tools may not understand GRE encapsulation or the TNI field, limiting their usefulness in troubleshooting and capacity planning. Scalable NVGRE environments require the deployment of advanced monitoring platforms that can decode GRE headers, interpret tenant identifiers, and correlate overlay activity with underlay performance metrics. Tools such as Microsoft Network Monitor, Wireshark with GRE support, and integrated solutions within System Center Operations Manager or Azure Monitor are essential for maintaining operational insight as the environment grows.

Automation and orchestration are crucial for managing NVGRE at scale. Manual configuration of virtual networks, address mappings, and gateway policies becomes unmanageable beyond a certain point. NVGRE environments integrated with SCVMM benefit from automation capabilities that enable dynamic provisioning of virtual networks, consistent policy enforcement, and responsive scaling of resources. Templates, scripts, and APIs allow administrators to define desired states and let the orchestration system handle the implementation and lifecycle management. This reduces configuration errors, accelerates deployment times, and supports rapid changes in response to shifting business or application demands.

Security and compliance must also scale with the network. As more tenants and virtual networks are added, the complexity of maintaining isolation and enforcing policies increases. NVGRE provides isolation through encapsulation and the use of unique TNIs, but additional security mechanisms are often required. Firewalls, access control lists, and network security groups must be applied in a consistent and automated way. Scalable environments often include centralized policy controllers that define and distribute security rules based on tenant context, workload type, or application function. These policies must be enforced across all NVGRE endpoints and gateways to maintain the integrity of the virtualized network.

NVGRE was designed with scalability in mind, and its architectural choices reflect a forward-looking approach to network virtualization. The use of GRE, the TNI, and integration with Hyper-V and SCVMM provide the foundational elements for building highly scalable multi-tenant networks. However, realizing this scalability in practice requires deliberate design, proper underlay configuration, efficient control plane management, and robust operational practices. As organizations adopt NVGRE to support increasingly complex and dynamic infrastructures, the ability to scale without sacrificing performance, visibility, or manageability remains a top priority and a central success factor in the long-term sustainability of the virtualized network fabric.

NVGRE Control Plane Options

The control plane in a network virtualization architecture is responsible for the distribution and synchronization of routing, forwarding, and endpoint information across the network fabric. In the context of NVGRE, or Network Virtualization using Generic Routing Encapsulation, the control plane assumes a particularly important role due to the encapsulated and abstracted nature of the network. While NVGRE is based on a simple and efficient encapsulation method using GRE, its control plane options are not as standardized or dynamic as those found in more modern overlay technologies like VXLAN with EVPN. This distinction has both advantages and limitations, especially in terms of scalability, automation, and operational complexity. Understanding the control plane options available for NVGRE is essential for designing a robust and manageable virtualized network environment.

NVGRE does not have a native, distributed control plane protocol built into its specification. This means that the forwarding information, such as mappings between virtual customer addresses and physical provider addresses, must be managed and disseminated using external mechanisms. Microsoft's implementation of NVGRE in Windows Server and System Center environments provides a centralized control plane model. In this model, the System Center Virtual Machine Manager, or SCVMM, acts as the authoritative source of network virtualization policies, including tenant network definitions, IP address assignments, and mapping of customer addresses to provider addresses. This central controller distributes the necessary information to each participating Hyper-V host, allowing them to construct the forwarding tables needed to encapsulate and route traffic across the NVGRE overlay.

The centralized control model used in NVGRE is tightly integrated with the Microsoft ecosystem. It leverages PowerShell scripts, configuration templates, and SCVMM APIs to create, update, and delete virtual networks and associated policies. When a new virtual machine is provisioned and assigned to a virtual network, SCVMM updates the corresponding Hyper-V hosts with the relevant policy data. This data includes the Tenant Network Identifier, or TNI, associated with the virtual subnet, the IP address assigned to the virtual machine, and the mapping of the customer IP to the host's provider address. These mappings are installed in the virtual switch on the Hyper-V host and are used to encapsulate traffic destined for other virtual machines within the same tenant network.

While the centralized approach simplifies deployment and ensures consistent policy enforcement, it can become a scalability bottleneck in very large environments. The reliance on SCVMM or other central policy servers introduces a single point of failure and may limit the speed at which updates can be propagated across the network. In environments with thousands of tenants and tens of thousands of virtual machines, the centralized control plane must be highly available, robust, and optimized for performance to prevent latency in policy application or stale forwarding entries. Failover, load balancing, and distributed instances of the policy engine may be necessary to maintain availability and responsiveness.

Another consideration in NVGRE control plane design is the need to manage customer-to-provider address translation. Because each virtual network is logically isolated and can use overlapping IP address space, the Hyper-V hosts must maintain accurate and up-to-date mappings for every customer IP in the environment. These mappings allow the virtual switch to encapsulate packets with the correct GRE header and route them to the destination host based on its provider IP address. The control plane is responsible for synchronizing these mappings and ensuring that they are removed or updated when virtual machines are moved, deleted, or reconfigured. In dynamic environments where workloads are frequently migrated or scaled, the responsiveness and accuracy of the control plane are critical for maintaining connectivity and performance.

In addition to static policy distribution via SCVMM, some deployments may implement custom control mechanisms using PowerShell automation or third-party orchestration platforms. These tools can interface with Hyper-V hosts directly and push configurations that define virtual networks, routing policies, and encapsulation parameters. While this approach offers flexibility and can reduce dependency on SCVMM, it also introduces complexity and requires careful coordination to avoid configuration drift or inconsistency. Custom control plane implementations must ensure atomicity, idempotence, and state reconciliation to avoid introducing network instability or misrouting.

Unlike VXLAN, which has adopted EVPN as a scalable, dynamic control plane for exchanging endpoint information using BGP, NVGRE does not support a distributed routing protocol for the exchange of customer or tenant route information. As a result, routing between virtual networks, and between virtual and physical networks, typically occurs through centralized gateway devices. These gateways maintain their own control plane, often using standard IP routing protocols such as BGP or OSPF, but do not participate in the NVGRE-specific control plane. This architectural separation means that routing and encapsulation functions are often decoupled, requiring careful design to ensure that routing policies align with encapsulation policies and that tenant isolation is maintained at both layers.

One potential approach to enhancing the control plane functionality in NVGRE is to combine it with a virtual network controller that abstracts the complexity of policy distribution and provides a more programmable interface for managing network state. Microsoft's Network Controller, introduced in later versions of Windows Server, offers such capabilities. It allows for centralized policy management, dynamic network topology discovery, and REST API-based orchestration. Although not tightly coupled to NVGRE in earlier implementations, the Network Controller represents a step toward a more modern control plane architecture that could eventually offer VXLAN-like flexibility to NVGRE networks.

Another aspect of control plane design in NVGRE is monitoring and diagnostics. Since NVGRE relies on encapsulation and logical separation, it is important to have visibility into the control plane state and ensure that mappings are correctly installed and synchronized. Tools such as Windows Event Viewer, PowerShell diagnostic cmdlets, and SCVMM dashboards provide insight into control plane health, including errors in policy distribution, stale address mappings, and misconfigurations. For advanced troubleshooting, administrators may also rely on packet captures and GRE-aware analyzers to trace encapsulated traffic and verify that TNI tagging and address translations are functioning correctly.

The evolution of network virtualization has shown that control plane design is just as important as data plane performance. NVGRE's control plane, while effective within the Microsoft ecosystem, lacks the dynamic peer-to-peer intelligence found in other overlay solutions. However, in controlled environments where Hyper-V and SCVMM are the standard, the centralized model can be sufficient and easier to manage, particularly when enhanced with automation, monitoring, and redundancy strategies. The long-term success of any NVGRE deployment depends on designing a control plane that not only supports current scalability and policy requirements but also adapts to future demands for agility, programmability, and interoperability.

NVGRE vs VXLAN: A Comparative View

NVGRE and VXLAN are two overlay network virtualization technologies that were developed to address the same fundamental challenge: how to create scalable, isolated, and flexible network environments in modern data centers and cloud architectures. Both were introduced as solutions to the limitations of traditional VLAN-based segmentation, particularly the 4096 VLAN ID restriction and the inability to extend Layer 2 networks across Layer 3 boundaries without complex configurations. While NVGRE and VXLAN share a common purpose, they differ in their technical implementations, ecosystem support, and long-term industry adoption. Comparing these two technologies across multiple dimensions reveals key distinctions that influence how they are deployed, managed, and scaled.

NVGRE, or Network Virtualization using Generic Routing Encapsulation, was developed primarily by Microsoft to integrate tightly with its Hyper-V virtualization platform. It uses GRE, a well-established tunneling protocol, to encapsulate Layer 2 Ethernet frames inside IP packets. VXLAN, or Virtual Extensible LAN, was developed jointly by VMware, Cisco, and Arista as a more vendor-neutral solution, using UDP-based encapsulation to achieve similar goals. Both technologies introduce a 24-bit identifier to support more than sixteen million isolated virtual networks, with NVGRE using the Tenant Network Identifier in the GRE key field and VXLAN using the VXLAN Network Identifier in its dedicated header.

One of the most significant differences between NVGRE and VXLAN lies in their encapsulation methods. NVGRE leverages GRE, which encapsulates packets directly over IP without a transport layer. This design reduces the encapsulation overhead slightly compared to VXLAN, which adds a UDP header and relies on Layer 4 ports. However, VXLAN's use of UDP has a notable advantage: it enables better load balancing across Equal-Cost Multi-Path routes in the underlay network. The UDP source port in VXLAN packets is typically generated using a hash of the inner packet headers, allowing network devices to distribute traffic more efficiently across multiple paths. In contrast, NVGRE's use of GRE, which lacks a transport layer, may lead to less optimal path utilization in ECMP environments unless additional configurations are introduced.

The control plane architecture also differentiates these two technologies. VXLAN originally relied on flood-and-learn mechanisms similar to traditional Ethernet switching. However, with the introduction of BGP EVPN as a standardized control plane, VXLAN deployments have become far more scalable and deterministic. EVPN allows dynamic exchange of MAC and IP address information across the VXLAN fabric, eliminating the need for broadcast-based discovery and enabling rapid convergence, mobility, and microsegmentation. NVGRE, by contrast, does not have a widely adopted distributed control plane. It typically depends on centralized policy servers, such as System Center Virtual Machine Manager in Microsoft environments, to manage customer-to-provider address mappings and network policies. This centralized model works well in tightly controlled environments but can become a bottleneck in large-scale, dynamic infrastructures where workloads and tenants are frequently added or moved.

Vendor and ecosystem support has played a critical role in the adoption trajectories of both technologies. VXLAN has seen broad support from networking vendors across the industry, including Cisco, Juniper, Arista, Dell, and VMware. It is natively supported in many data center switches, hypervisors, and network interface cards, making it a preferred choice for multi-vendor environments and large-scale cloud providers. NVGRE, while supported in Microsoft Hyper-V and integrated into the Windows Server ecosystem, has a narrower vendor footprint. Its adoption outside Microsoft-centric environments has been limited, in part due to the lack of hardware acceleration and native support in third-party network devices.

Operationally, VXLAN is often seen as more flexible due to its hardware offload capabilities and standardized telemetry options. Many modern NICs support VXLAN offload, allowing encapsulation and decapsulation to be handled in silicon rather than software, which improves performance and reduces CPU usage on hypervisors. VXLAN also integrates more easily with telemetry and analytics platforms that can parse UDP and VXLAN headers to provide visibility into tenant traffic and overlay behavior. NVGRE, while supported in some offload-capable NICs, has fewer options for hardware-based acceleration and requires more manual effort to achieve equivalent observability in large environments.

From a deployment perspective, NVGRE is generally simpler to set up in Microsoft environments due to its native integration with Windows Server and SCVMM. Administrators can define virtual networks, assign IP pools, and configure gateway access through familiar management interfaces and automation scripts. This ease of use is an advantage in private cloud scenarios where Hyper-V is the standard virtualization platform. VXLAN, while more complex to configure in its early stages, has matured significantly with the advent of EVPN, intent-based networking, and automated fabric provisioning tools. Network operators can now deploy VXLAN fabrics using controller-based architectures that offer lifecycle management, policy enforcement, and integration with cloud-native orchestrators.

Security and multi-tenancy are core use cases for both technologies, and each provides mechanisms for tenant isolation. NVGRE uses the TNI to keep tenant traffic separate, allowing each tenant to operate with its own addressing scheme. VXLAN does the same with its VNI and, when combined with EVPN, offers additional policy granularity for securing inter-tenant traffic and enforcing segmentation rules. VXLAN's broader toolset for microsegmentation and policy-based routing has made it more suitable for zero-trust architectures and environments where fine-grained security is a priority.

In terms of future outlook, VXLAN has gained momentum as the de facto standard for network virtualization in cloud-scale data centers. Its widespread industry support, integration with EVPN, and flexibility in mixed-vendor environments have made it the preferred choice for new deployments. NVGRE, while still functional and relevant in Microsoft-centric infrastructures, is increasingly seen as a transitional technology that paved the way for more modern solutions. Microsoft itself has moved toward supporting VXLAN in its Azure cloud platform and newer SDN implementations, signaling a broader shift in direction.

Ultimately, the choice between NVGRE and VXLAN depends on the specific needs of the environment, existing infrastructure investments, and long-term goals. NVGRE provides a well-integrated solution for organizations standardized on Hyper-V and Microsoft's virtualization stack, offering ease of use and simplified management. VXLAN, with its ecosystem flexibility, advanced control plane, and high scalability, offers a more robust foundation for large, dynamic, and heterogeneous data centers. Understanding the technical and operational trade-offs between the two allows network architects to make informed decisions that align with their performance, security, and automation requirements. Each technology represents a step in the evolution of network virtualization, reflecting different philosophies and approaches to building the data center networks of the future.

Introduction to GENEVE

GENEVE, which stands for Generic Network Virtualization Encapsulation, is a modern network virtualization protocol designed to address the limitations and operational gaps found in earlier tunneling technologies such as VXLAN and NVGRE. As data centers evolved to become more dynamic, distributed, and heavily reliant on virtualization and software-defined networking, the need for a more extensible and adaptable encapsulation format became clear. GENEVE was developed as a collaborative effort through the Internet Engineering Task Force (IETF) with the specific goal of combining the strengths of existing overlay technologies while introducing a level of flexibility and extensibility that allows it to evolve alongside emerging requirements. GENEVE is not just another tunneling protocol; it is an attempt to unify and standardize how virtual networks are encapsulated and carried over IP fabrics, while providing a flexible metadata framework that can support a wide variety of use cases without requiring protocol redesign.

One of the primary motivations behind GENEVE was the realization that earlier overlay technologies had become increasingly feature-limited as new network and application requirements emerged. VXLAN, while widely adopted and supported in hardware, has a fixed header structure that restricts the type and amount of information that can be included in the encapsulated packet. NVGRE also suffers from limitations in extensibility and is closely tied to specific vendor ecosystems, making it less suitable for highly programmable and cloud-native environments. GENEVE, on the other hand, introduces a flexible and extensible metadata model that allows operators and developers to insert custom information into the packet header through a modular options field. This capability is particularly valuable in environments where policy enforcement, telemetry, service chaining, or traffic steering depend on context that cannot be conveyed using traditional fixed header fields.

The encapsulation mechanism of GENEVE closely resembles that of VXLAN in its use of UDP as the transport protocol. This design choice was made to ensure compatibility with existing IP networks and to support equal-cost multi-path routing through entropy in the UDP source port field. Like VXLAN, GENEVE encapsulates Layer 2 Ethernet frames within a UDP/IP packet, allowing virtual networks to span Layer 3 boundaries and interconnect endpoints across different physical locations. The outer IP and UDP headers are used to route the packet between tunnel endpoints, while the GENEVE header carries information necessary to re-establish the logical context at the receiving end. However, where GENEVE significantly diverges is in the structure and functionality of its header.

The GENEVE header includes a version field, a control bits section, a 24-bit Virtual Network Identifier (VNI), and an options field of variable length. The VNI provides network segmentation and supports over sixteen million virtual networks, similar to VXLAN and NVGRE. The real innovation lies in the options field, which allows the inclusion of arbitrary metadata using a Type-Length-Value format. These options are not predefined or static; instead, they are registered through IETF-managed registries and can be vendor-specific, controller-defined, or universally agreed upon. This model allows GENEVE to support evolving needs such as security group tagging, identity propagation, flow tracking, or even specific application or workload context, all without altering the base protocol.

The extensibility of GENEVE also has significant implications for software-defined networking. In SDN environments, centralized controllers make decisions based on detailed network state and traffic context. GENEVE enables these controllers to embed this context directly into the packet, allowing network devices to execute forwarding or policy decisions without relying on external lookups. This capability supports more efficient and scalable implementations of features like service function chaining, where traffic must be steered through a series of network functions, each of which may apply policies or transformations based on metadata carried in the packet itself. The ability to insert, read, and act upon such metadata directly at the data plane level gives GENEVE a distinct advantage in programmable networks.

While GENEVE's architecture is highly forward-looking, it also considers performance and hardware compatibility. The protocol is designed to be simple enough for implementation in hardware, although its extensibility features are more naturally aligned with software-based processing. Many modern network interface cards and switches are beginning to support GENEVE offloads, and the protocol has been adopted by several open-source projects such as Open vSwitch and OpenStack, further demonstrating its growing traction. Hardware vendors are increasingly recognizing the value of GENEVE's flexibility and are working toward integrating support for common use cases where header parsing and actions can be standardized.

From a deployment perspective, GENEVE can coexist with other overlay technologies, allowing gradual migration or hybrid environments where different tunneling protocols serve specific roles. Organizations adopting GENEVE typically do so to future-proof their networks and align with more software-defined, API-driven approaches to infrastructure management. The protocol's ability to accommodate new metadata types without redesign makes it especially attractive in multi-tenant environments, edge computing scenarios, and cloud-native applications where agility and observability are paramount.

GENEVE's ability to encapsulate not just traffic but also intent represents a major shift in how overlay networks can be designed and operated. In traditional overlays, forwarding decisions are often made based solely on destination addresses and static policies. GENEVE enables those decisions to be made dynamically and with full awareness of the flow's context, making it possible to build smarter, more adaptive networks. Whether used for enforcing security policies, collecting detailed telemetry data, or orchestrating traffic through complex service chains, the protocol supports an unprecedented degree of customization.

As the networking landscape continues to evolve, with trends like containerization, microservices, and edge computing becoming dominant, the need for a versatile and extensible tunneling mechanism becomes more urgent. GENEVE is positioned to meet this demand not only through its technical features but also through its open and collaborative development model. By embracing flexibility, extensibility, and interoperability, GENEVE represents a convergence of the lessons learned from VXLAN and NVGRE, while providing a platform that can grow alongside the needs of cloud-native and software-defined infrastructure. The result is a protocol that not only meets the demands of today's data centers but is also equipped to adapt to the complex, dynamic, and diverse requirements of tomorrow's networks.

GENEVE Design Goals and Motivation

The emergence of GENEVE as a network virtualization protocol is rooted in the growing complexity and dynamism of modern data center and cloud networks. As the limitations of previous tunneling protocols such as VXLAN and NVGRE became more evident, it was clear that the industry required a more flexible, extensible, and future-proof solution. The design goals and motivations behind GENEVE reflect an attempt to address these deficiencies by creating a protocol that is not bound by rigid header structures or constrained feature sets. Instead, GENEVE was envisioned as a unifying overlay encapsulation method capable of evolving alongside networking requirements, operational models, and application architectures. The goal was not just to build another encapsulation protocol but to design a foundation for modern software-defined networking, cloud-native infrastructure, and highly programmable environments.

A key motivation in the development of GENEVE was the recognition that static header formats inherently limit a protocol's adaptability. VXLAN, for instance, introduced a fixed header structure with a 24-bit VXLAN Network Identifier and no native support for additional metadata. While this design served well for basic Layer 2 network virtualization, it proved inadequate when operators and developers needed to embed context-aware information such as tenant identity, security tags, quality-of-service markings, or telemetry data. These types of metadata became increasingly important in cloud environments where automation, multi-tenancy, and service chaining required packets to carry more than just routing and addressing information. The inability to extend VXLAN without redefining the protocol itself led to fragmentation and proprietary extensions. GENEVE was therefore conceived as a framework that could include additional information in a structured and standardized way, without breaking backward compatibility or requiring protocol redesign.

Another significant design objective of GENEVE was to unify the diverse overlay encapsulation practices used across the industry. Different vendors and platforms had implemented their own variations of overlay tunneling to meet specific goals. This resulted in operational inconsistencies, limited interoperability, and complexity in multi-vendor deployments. GENEVE was developed through a collaborative effort within the IETF, with input from many leading vendors and open-source projects, including VMware, Microsoft, and Red Hat. The intent was to create a protocol that could serve as a common denominator for overlay networking, allowing both hardware and software implementations to interoperate while supporting a wide range of use cases. By standardizing the encapsulation format and offering a structured mechanism for extensibility, GENEVE enables a consistent operational model that reduces the need for vendor-specific solutions.

Scalability was another foundational goal for GENEVE. As data centers scaled to support tens of thousands of tenants and millions of workloads, network virtualization protocols needed to ensure minimal overhead while maximizing efficiency. GENEVE retains the use of the 24-bit Virtual Network Identifier, consistent with VXLAN and NVGRE, enabling over 16 million isolated segments. This vast namespace allows cloud providers and large enterprises to assign each tenant, department, or application its own virtual network without concern for resource exhaustion. However, GENEVE also goes beyond simply scaling the number of network segments. Its support for variable-length option fields allows rich policy data to be carried in the packet itself, making it easier to implement granular access control, traffic steering, and routing decisions in a distributed and scalable manner. These options can be tailored to the specific needs of each network without requiring changes to the base protocol, enabling an unprecedented degree of customization.

Flexibility in deployment and implementation was also a major motivation behind GENEVE. One of the criticisms of earlier protocols was their inflexibility in adapting to new transport technologies or deployment environments. VXLAN, for instance, mandates the use of UDP, which is well suited for ECMP and broad hardware support but may not always be optimal in every context. GENEVE is transport agnostic by design, allowing encapsulated packets to be carried over

UDP, TCP, or other transport mechanisms depending on the needs of the deployment. This abstraction enables future use cases such as secure transport over TLS, optimized delivery over RDMA, or other transport-layer innovations. The ability to evolve transport options without altering the encapsulation header itself makes GENEVE well positioned for long-term adaptability.

Another design goal of GENEVE was to better support network programmability and automation, particularly in software-defined networking architectures. In SDN models, the control plane is logically centralized, making decisions based on global network state, while the data plane enforces those decisions based on packet attributes. GENEVE's extensible option fields allow controllers to encode rich policy metadata directly into packets. This approach supports intelligent forwarding decisions, dynamic service chaining, and real-time enforcement of security policies without requiring additional lookup tables or external stateful processing. Because these policies travel with the packet, they reduce the burden on intermediate devices and allow a more distributed, stateless, and scalable enforcement model.

Security and observability were also critical considerations in the design of GENEVE. As data centers became more distributed and tenant isolation more critical, the ability to track and enforce security boundaries at a granular level became essential. GENEVE enables each packet to carry contextual information such as tenant identity, application role, or trust level. This information can be used by security appliances or virtual firewalls to make decisions on packet inspection or filtering. Furthermore, GENEVE's support for extensible telemetry options allows detailed monitoring information to be embedded in the data stream, facilitating real-time analytics and troubleshooting. Network administrators can extract flow-specific metrics, track path selection, or correlate packet behavior across overlay and underlay networks without relying entirely on external monitoring infrastructure.

Compatibility with hardware was also a guiding principle in GENEVE's development. While the protocol was designed to enable rich metadata in software environments, it also includes design constraints that make it feasible for hardware implementation. Common options and behaviors can be standardized to allow silicon vendors to build parsing and processing capabilities into network interface cards and switches. This ensures that GENEVE can scale not only in terms of functionality but also in terms of performance, meeting the high-throughput requirements of production data centers without sacrificing visibility or programmability.

In summary, GENEVE's design goals and motivations reflect a deep understanding of the evolving challenges in network virtualization. It is not a reactionary protocol, but rather a forward-looking foundation built to support the current and future needs of cloud-scale, software-defined, and programmable networks. By addressing the rigidity, fragmentation, and operational limitations of its predecessors, GENEVE establishes itself as a protocol that can adapt, scale, and unify the diverse networking requirements of modern infrastructure while enabling innovation at every layer of the network stack.

GENEVE Header and Metadata Flexibility

The GENEVE protocol was conceived to address the shortcomings of earlier network virtualization overlay technologies, particularly regarding extensibility, programmability, and operational efficiency. Central to its innovation is the structure and flexibility of the GENEVE header, which was designed with the foresight that modern and future networking environments require more than simple encapsulation of Ethernet frames over IP. The GENEVE header introduces a modular, extensible format that not only carries the essential information needed for tunneling and segmentation but also allows for a wide range of metadata to be embedded within the packet. This capability transforms GENEVE from a basic encapsulation method into a dynamic, programmable framework capable of supporting the demands of software-defined networking, telemetry, service chaining, and policy-driven infrastructure.

The standard GENEVE header includes a fixed portion that contains core tunneling information such as the version, critical flags, protocol type, and the Virtual Network Identifier. This portion of the header is designed to provide just enough fixed structure to ensure interoperability and efficient packet processing, while avoiding the rigidity that has limited the evolution of other tunneling protocols. The version field, currently set to zero, allows for forward compatibility by providing a mechanism to introduce future versions of the protocol without disrupting existing implementations. The critical flags field indicates whether certain options included in the packet must be understood and processed by the receiving endpoint, allowing senders to indicate which metadata is essential and which can be safely ignored by intermediate devices.

One of the defining components of the GENEVE header is the 24-bit Virtual Network Identifier, or VNI. This field, much like the VXLAN Network Identifier or NVGRE's Tenant Network Identifier, provides the logical segmentation necessary to distinguish one virtual network from another. With over sixteen million possible values, the VNI supports highly scalable multi-tenant environments, enabling isolation between different tenants or applications running on shared physical infrastructure. The VNI ensures that virtual machines, containers, or other workloads remain within their designated virtual network context, regardless of their physical location within the data center.

However, the most powerful and innovative aspect of the GENEVE header lies in its extensible options field. This field allows the inclusion of metadata in the form of Type-Length-Value elements, where each option consists of a defined type identifier, a length descriptor, and the actual data. This design allows GENEVE to carry not only tunneling information but also any arbitrary context required by the control plane, management tools, or security policies. The protocol does not impose a strict limit on the number or type of options that can be included, offering a highly flexible and customizable metadata transport mechanism. This flexibility enables GENEVE to support use cases that were previously impossible or required proprietary extensions in other overlay protocols.

Each GENEVE option type is defined through an IETF-managed registry, ensuring standardized behavior across implementations while also allowing room for vendor-specific or experimental extensions. The types can represent a wide variety of data, such as tenant identifiers, application-specific flags, quality-of-service settings, traffic classification tags, or encryption parameters. For example, a service provider might use GENEVE options to encode subscriber identifiers, allowing edge devices to enforce policies based on customer identity. A cloud platform might encode security group information to enforce firewall rules or carry telemetry data that facilitates flow-based analytics. These option types are processed by devices that recognize them and ignored by those that do not, preserving backward compatibility while enabling incremental feature deployment.

The ability to carry metadata directly within the encapsulated packet also enhances the performance and scalability of network services. In traditional overlay networks, context-aware forwarding or policy enforcement often requires additional state to be maintained in external databases or network controllers. GENEVE's metadata model allows this context to travel with the packet itself, enabling devices in the data path to make decisions without consulting external sources. This reduces latency, improves resilience, and enables stateless operation for intermediate devices, which is particularly valuable in large-scale or distributed network environments.

Another benefit of GENEVE's metadata flexibility is its support for service function chaining. In complex networks, packets may need to traverse a sequence of services such as firewalls, load balancers, or intrusion detection systems. Each service may need to inspect or modify the packet based on certain metadata. With GENEVE, service identifiers, state indicators, or policy directives can be encoded as options, allowing each service in the chain to interpret and act upon the information as needed. This facilitates precise traffic steering and consistent policy enforcement across multiple stages of the service chain, without relying on external orchestration for every hop.

GENEVE's header structure also contributes to enhanced observability and diagnostics. Network administrators can insert telemetry options that record timestamps, path traces, or performance indicators. These options can be sampled or analyzed in real time, providing deep insight into network behavior without requiring external probes or duplicated flows. This approach to embedded observability supports advanced use cases like intent-based networking, where the network must continuously verify that it is behaving according to operator-defined goals and policies.

Despite its extensibility, the GENEVE header remains efficient and compatible with modern hardware. Common options can be standardized and implemented in silicon, allowing for high-performance packet processing in network interface cards or top-of-rack switches. At the same time, software implementations can handle less frequent or more complex options, providing a balance between speed and flexibility. This hybrid model ensures that GENEVE can scale in both enterprise and cloud environments while supporting innovation at the data plane level.

The architecture of the GENEVE header reflects a conscious departure from the limitations of fixed-format tunneling protocols. It embraces the principles of openness, extensibility, and programmability, allowing network operators, cloud providers, and developers to define their own semantics, insert dynamic context, and evolve their networks without waiting for protocol standardization. As networks continue to become more software-driven and workload-centric, the need for such flexibility becomes not only advantageous but essential. GENEVE's ability to support arbitrary metadata within its header ensures it can meet a wide range of current and future requirements, making it a foundational protocol for modern, adaptive, and intelligent networking infrastructures.

GENEVE in OpenStack and Cloud Platforms

GENEVE has emerged as one of the most promising encapsulation protocols in modern cloud networking due to its extensibility, flexibility, and alignment with the needs of software-defined infrastructure. Its integration into OpenStack and other cloud platforms represents a key step in the evolution of overlay networking within multi-tenant, dynamic, and scalable environments. As traditional tunneling protocols such as VXLAN and NVGRE began to show limitations in extensibility and metadata transport, cloud platforms required a new method to support context-aware networking, automation, and service chaining. GENEVE addresses these needs by introducing a protocol capable of not only transporting packets but also conveying application, policy, and service-level information directly within the packet header.

In the context of OpenStack, the networking component known as Neutron is responsible for managing the creation and orchestration of virtual networks, routers, and security policies. OpenStack Neutron has traditionally supported VXLAN as the default tunneling mechanism for tenant isolation. However, as OpenStack environments have grown in complexity, the need for greater visibility and control over network flows has increased. GENEVE provides a more suitable alternative due to its ability to embed arbitrary metadata as Type-Length-Value (TLV) options in the encapsulation header. This capability allows OpenStack to carry information such as security group IDs, tenant identifiers, quality-of-service tags, or service path indexes directly within the data plane, eliminating the need for separate control messages or stateful lookup tables.

One of the most notable implementations of GENEVE in the OpenStack ecosystem is through Open vSwitch, a multilayer virtual switch that plays a central role in OpenStack networking deployments. Open vSwitch, often referred to as OVS, serves as the virtual switch used by hypervisors to bridge virtual machine interfaces to physical networks. OVS has added support for GENEVE as a native tunneling option, allowing OpenStack administrators to define overlay networks that use GENEVE for encapsulation. This support is particularly significant because OVS also includes the OpenFlow protocol for fine-grained traffic control and integrates with controllers such as OpenDaylight and OVN (Open Virtual Network). The ability of OVS to parse and act on GENEVE option metadata allows cloud platforms to build intelligent data paths that can adapt to changing policies and tenant configurations in real time.

OVN, a subproject of the Open vSwitch initiative, is designed to provide virtual network abstraction and control to OpenStack and Kubernetes environments. It acts as a controller that manages logical network topologies and translates them into flow rules on OVS-based datapaths. OVN has adopted GENEVE as its preferred tunneling protocol because of its flexibility in metadata transport. With GENEVE, OVN can encode logical port identifiers, MAC bindings, load balancing hints, and other policy data directly in the packet. This design simplifies the controller logic by reducing reliance on external databases and enables faster convergence during topology changes or policy updates. GENEVE's metadata extensibility is leveraged in OVN to maintain a distributed and scalable overlay network that supports rich tenant isolation and dynamic provisioning.

Beyond OpenStack, GENEVE is gaining traction in broader cloud-native and containerized environments. As more workloads migrate to Kubernetes-based platforms, the demand for flexible and programmable networking protocols continues to rise. Container orchestrators often require the network to support microsegmentation, dynamic service discovery, traffic steering, and detailed telemetry—all of which align closely with GENEVE's design. GENEVE's ability to encode metadata such as namespace labels, pod identities, or service chains makes it an ideal candidate for use in container networking plugins (CNI) and service mesh architectures. Integrations between Kubernetes and OVN further highlight GENEVE's role as the next-generation overlay protocol for cloud-native infrastructure.

In large public or private clouds, where multitenancy and self-service provisioning are essential, GENEVE also enables greater security and operational insight. By carrying context-aware metadata, network devices and security appliances can enforce policies based on the identity and role of the workload rather than just IP or MAC addresses. For example, security groups or firewall rules can be enforced using metadata fields that indicate the tenant, application tier, or compliance domain of the traffic. This approach supports more granular and dynamic policy enforcement, which is critical in multi-tenant environments where network boundaries and application compositions are constantly changing.

The adoption of GENEVE in cloud platforms also enhances observability and troubleshooting. By embedding telemetry data or tracing information in packet headers, operators can monitor flows, measure latency, and track path decisions without relying solely on external agents or packet mirroring. This improves the ability of cloud platforms to implement features such as flow analytics, service-level agreement monitoring, and anomaly detection. It also facilitates intent-based networking strategies, where the network continuously validates that it is operating according to the desired state defined by administrators or automated systems.

Hardware compatibility has been an important factor in making GENEVE viable in production cloud environments. While initial implementations of GENEVE were software-based, growing support from network interface card vendors and switch manufacturers has made hardware offloading feasible. Smart NICs and programmable switches are beginning to support parsing and processing of GENEVE headers and common metadata options. This enables cloud platforms to offload encapsulation and metadata inspection from the CPU to dedicated hardware, improving performance and reducing the impact on compute resources. The combination of software flexibility and hardware acceleration positions GENEVE as an efficient and scalable solution for high-throughput cloud environments.

The evolution of cloud platforms from monolithic to distributed, microservices-based architectures has placed new demands on the network. These demands include tenant-aware routing, real-time security enforcement, automated service insertion, and deep telemetry. GENEVE's role in meeting these demands within OpenStack and other cloud platforms continues to grow. Its design as a generic and extensible encapsulation protocol makes it suitable for a wide range of use cases, from simple tenant isolation to complex service chaining and policy enforcement. Its ability to carry rich metadata within each packet enables a new level of intelligence in the data plane, empowering cloud networks to become more adaptive, responsive, and programmable. Through projects like Open vSwitch, OVN, and OpenStack Neutron, GENEVE is not just a tunneling format but a foundational technology enabling the next generation of cloud networking.

GENEVE Controller-Based Deployments

GENEVE was created with a flexible and extensible architecture to support the demands of dynamic, programmable networks, and one of its most powerful use cases is in controller-based deployments. These deployments are central to the operation of modern software-defined networks, where control logic is separated from the data forwarding plane and centralized in one or more controllers that orchestrate the behavior of the entire fabric. GENEVE fits naturally into this paradigm because of its ability to carry rich metadata directly in the encapsulation header, enabling centralized controllers to define complex forwarding behaviors and security policies that can be implemented consistently across a distributed network infrastructure.

In controller-based deployments, the GENEVE tunnel endpoints—often virtual switches, smart NICs, or physical top-of-rack switches—are controlled by a logically centralized controller that manages the network state, computes forwarding paths, and installs flow rules. The controller uses its global view of the network to make intelligent decisions, such as how to handle new flows, how to segment tenants, and how to enforce policies. These decisions are translated into flow rules and sent to the tunnel endpoints through protocols such as OpenFlow, OVSDB, or gRPC depending on the architecture of the deployment. GENEVE's design enables the controller to embed critical context into each packet, such as tenant identifiers, application labels, service chaining information, or even telemetry markers, all through its extensible metadata model.

One of the key advantages of controller-based deployments using GENEVE is the efficiency with which policies can be enforced. Traditional distributed routing or switching environments often require extensive per-node configuration and coordination to maintain consistency across the fabric. With GENEVE and a centralized controller, policies such as segmentation, access control, or traffic steering can be defined once and propagated uniformly across the network. This model supports agile network provisioning and makes it possible to spin up isolated tenant environments or secure application tiers in seconds. The controller manages the Virtual Network Identifier space and assigns VNIs to virtual networks dynamically, reducing the risk of conflicts and enabling true multi-tenancy at scale.

Another important benefit is the simplification of service chaining, which is the process of directing traffic through a sequence of middleboxes or virtualized network functions such as firewalls, load balancers, intrusion detection systems, or WAN optimizers. In traditional networks, service chaining requires complex route manipulation or manual path configuration. In a GENEVE-enabled controller-based deployment, the controller can simply add metadata options to the GENEVE header to encode the desired service path. Each network function in the chain can inspect the header, determine its place in the sequence, and act accordingly. This stateless and dynamic approach allows services to be inserted or removed from chains without disrupting active flows, supporting on-demand service deployment and elastic scaling of network functions.

The metadata flexibility offered by GENEVE is especially valuable in environments where fine-grained context is needed to apply differentiated policies. A controller can encode a wide range of attributes in the GENEVE options field, such as user role, application ID, or threat level. Network devices receiving these packets can then apply forwarding or filtering decisions based not only on Layer 2 or Layer 3 headers but on rich Layer 7-aware context. This capability enables intent-based networking, where the network automatically adapts to the desired state defined by business or operational objectives, instead of relying on manual configurations and static rules.

Controller-based deployments with GENEVE are also well-suited for hybrid and multi-cloud environments, where consistent policy enforcement and network segmentation must be maintained across geographically dispersed and heterogeneous infrastructures. A centralized controller can orchestrate GENEVE tunnel creation between different cloud regions or on-premises sites and manage the dissemination of policy and forwarding information. By encapsulating traffic in GENEVE and including metadata that travels with each packet, the network can maintain tenant isolation, enforce security policies, and optimize traffic flows regardless of physical location. This is critical for organizations operating at global scale, where applications and users span multiple environments.

Performance and observability are also enhanced in GENEVE controller-based deployments. Because the controller has full visibility into network topology and flow state, it can perform traffic engineering functions such as path optimization, load balancing, and congestion avoidance. It can also collect telemetry data from tunnel endpoints, analyze traffic patterns, and adjust forwarding behavior in real time. The GENEVE protocol itself supports the inclusion of telemetry data directly in the encapsulated packets, allowing in-band collection of performance metrics such as latency, hop count, and loss rate. This reduces the need for out-of-band monitoring systems and supports closed-loop automation, where network behavior is continuously monitored and adjusted to meet service level objectives.

Security is another area where controller-based GENEVE deployments provide significant benefits. The controller can enforce global access control policies and microsegmentation rules by embedding security group identifiers or trust levels into the GENEVE metadata. Network devices at the edge of the overlay can read these values and enforce policies without maintaining large local state tables. Additionally, GENEVE packets can be authenticated and encrypted using secure transport mechanisms, such as IPsec or TLS, further enhancing the confidentiality and integrity of tenant traffic. This centralized policy enforcement model simplifies compliance and auditing, making it easier to demonstrate security posture to internal stakeholders and external regulators.

The flexibility of the GENEVE header also facilitates rapid innovation in controller-based networks. As new requirements emerge—such as support for 5G network slicing, IoT segmentation, or AI-driven traffic analysis—the protocol can evolve through the introduction of new option types. Because these options are encoded in a standard Type-Length-Value format, new functionalities can be deployed incrementally without disrupting existing infrastructure. This extensibility future-proofs the network and reduces the lifecycle cost of deploying new services or adapting to evolving business needs.

In practice, many organizations are already leveraging GENEVE in controller-based environments through projects like Open Virtual Network (OVN), which uses Open vSwitch and integrates tightly with orchestration platforms such as OpenStack and Kubernetes. These implementations demonstrate the viability and effectiveness of GENEVE as the overlay protocol of choice for programmable and scalable cloud networks. With its rich metadata capabilities and compatibility with centralized control architectures, GENEVE enables networks to become more responsive, secure, and adaptable than ever before. As controller-based networking continues to gain traction in both enterprise and cloud contexts, GENEVE stands out as a protocol designed not only for today's demands but also for the evolving challenges of next-generation infrastructure.

GENEVE Performance and Optimization

The adoption of GENEVE in data centers and cloud networks has introduced significant flexibility and extensibility to the realm of network virtualization. However, beyond its architectural elegance and support for advanced metadata handling, it is essential to analyze the protocol's impact on performance and understand how to optimize its deployment for high-throughput, low-latency environments. GENEVE was designed not only to be adaptable and programmable but also to function efficiently in a variety of workloads ranging from tenant isolation in public clouds to fine-grained traffic steering in service provider networks. Its performance characteristics depend heavily on both the software and hardware implementations, and understanding the mechanisms that influence its behavior is crucial for achieving optimal results in production deployments.

One of the most immediate performance considerations in any encapsulation protocol is the overhead introduced by tunneling. GENEVE adds an encapsulation header composed of fixed fields and optional metadata, in addition to the standard outer UDP and IP headers. While the base header is relatively lightweight, the inclusion of multiple metadata options can significantly increase the total packet size. This additional overhead means that encapsulated packets may exceed the standard Ethernet maximum transmission unit, which is typically 1500 bytes. In high-performance environments, it is necessary to enable jumbo frames throughout the network to accommodate these larger packets. Without appropriate MTU configuration, fragmentation may occur, leading to increased latency, higher CPU utilization, and reduced throughput.

Another important aspect of GENEVE performance is its reliance on UDP for transport. UDP was chosen in part to facilitate equal-cost multi-path routing across IP networks, which distributes traffic across multiple paths and maximizes available bandwidth. This characteristic is especially beneficial in leaf-spine data center topologies, where multiple uplinks exist between switches and the efficient use of all links is crucial. However, while UDP is well-suited for multipathing, it lacks the congestion control and reliability features of TCP. Therefore, ensuring that the underlay network is well-provisioned, low-latency, and free from packet loss is essential for consistent GENEVE performance. UDP-based transport also interacts well with existing flow hashing algorithms in hardware switches, enabling balanced load distribution without requiring deep packet inspection.

CPU performance is a major factor in the deployment of GENEVE, particularly when the protocol is implemented in software, as is common in many virtual switches like Open vSwitch. The processes of encapsulating and decapsulating packets, parsing metadata, and applying policy decisions can consume significant processing resources. In high-density virtual environments, the cumulative effect of per-packet processing can lead to bottlenecks. To mitigate this, performance optimization strategies often include the use of Data Plane Development Kit (DPDK), which provides high-performance packet processing capabilities in user space, bypassing the traditional kernel networking stack. DPDK allows applications to achieve much higher throughput and lower latency, making it a key enabler of efficient GENEVE deployments in software-based switches.

Beyond software optimization, hardware acceleration plays a crucial role in scaling GENEVE networks. Modern network interface cards and smart NICs increasingly offer offload capabilities for encapsulation protocols. When GENEVE support is implemented in hardware, the NIC can perform encapsulation and decapsulation tasks, as well as some option parsing, without involving the CPU. This frees up host resources for applications and significantly reduces latency and jitter. To fully take advantage of hardware offload, it is necessary to ensure that both the NIC and its drivers support GENEVE natively, and that the hypervisor or operating system is configured to offload relevant tasks to the hardware. When properly configured, this can lead to near-line-rate performance even in highly virtualized environments with complex networking requirements.

Another critical area of GENEVE performance tuning involves the use of metadata. While GENEVE's extensible metadata is one of its strongest features, excessive or inefficient use of custom options can degrade performance. Parsing long option lists adds processing overhead at each tunnel endpoint and may require additional memory accesses or lookup operations. To optimize performance, it is important to carefully design metadata structures, limit the use of unnecessary options, and align option lengths to word boundaries to facilitate efficient parsing. In some cases, common options can be standardized and implemented directly in hardware, allowing rapid decision-making and policy enforcement without involving general-purpose processing logic.

Scalability is also a major concern in GENEVE-based networks. As the number of tunnels and endpoints increases, the overhead of maintaining tunnel state, forwarding tables, and policy mappings grows. To address this, centralized controllers or distributed databases can be used to manage tunnel lifecycle and synchronize endpoint information. Control plane optimization ensures that tunnel setup and teardown do not introduce unnecessary delays and that policy updates propagate quickly across the network. This is especially important in cloud environments where virtual machines and containers are frequently created, migrated, or destroyed. Fast convergence and minimal downtime are essential to maintaining high availability and service continuity.

Telemetry and observability are increasingly important components of performance optimization in GENEVE networks. By embedding telemetry information in GENEVE metadata fields, operators can gain real-time insights into packet flow, latency, loss, and routing decisions. These insights enable proactive performance tuning, anomaly detection, and capacity planning. GENEVE supports the inclusion of in-band telemetry markers that travel with the packet, allowing network devices to append or update performance data as the packet traverses the infrastructure. When combined with advanced analytics platforms, this capability enables closed-loop performance management and rapid identification of bottlenecks or misconfigurations.

Security features also affect performance, particularly when encryption, authentication, or policy enforcement are applied to tunneled traffic. While GENEVE itself does not mandate encryption, many deployments secure overlay traffic using IPsec, TLS, or MACsec depending on the transport environment. These security layers introduce computational overhead and can impact throughput if not properly offloaded or scaled. Hardware-based encryption modules, dedicated security appliances, or smart NICs with inline crypto engines can mitigate this impact and allow secure, high-speed transport of GENEVE-encapsulated traffic across shared or untrusted networks.

Integration with container orchestration platforms also introduces performance considerations. In Kubernetes environments, for instance, GENEVE may be used in conjunction with container networking interfaces or service meshes. These deployments require rapid provisioning and high pod density, which can challenge the overlay's scalability and processing capacity. Fine-tuning GENEVE performance in these scenarios involves optimizing the container network plugin, ensuring efficient tunnel reuse, and minimizing the number of unique metadata variants to reduce parsing complexity.

Ultimately, GENEVE's performance depends on a careful balance between flexibility and efficiency. Its extensible architecture allows it to support a wide array of use cases, but realizing its full potential in production requires thoughtful design and tuning. Whether deployed in a virtualized data center, cloud-native platform, or multi-tenant service provider environment, the key to GENEVE performance lies in aligning protocol capabilities with hardware acceleration, software optimization, and intelligent control plane design. When these elements are properly integrated, GENEVE can deliver high-speed, context-aware networking that meets the demands of modern applications without compromising on agility, observability, or scalability.

Comparing GENEVE to VXLAN and NVGRE

Overlay networking protocols have become essential components of modern data center and cloud infrastructure, enabling scalable network virtualization and tenant isolation across shared physical environments. Among the most widely discussed and implemented encapsulation protocols are VXLAN, NVGRE, and GENEVE. Each of these protocols was developed in response to the growing limitations of traditional VLAN-based segmentation, and each reflects different design philosophies, technical priorities, and deployment strategies. While all three achieve the core objective of encapsulating Layer 2 frames for transport over IP-based Layer 3 networks, their architectural differences have significant implications for scalability, flexibility, performance, interoperability, and long-term viability.

VXLAN, or Virtual Extensible LAN, was one of the earliest successful attempts to solve the scalability limitations of VLANs. By introducing a 24-bit VXLAN Network Identifier, VXLAN increased the number of available virtual networks from the 4096 allowed by VLANs to over sixteen million. This change made it possible to support thousands of tenants and workloads in cloud-scale environments. VXLAN uses UDP for encapsulation, allowing for better compatibility with Equal-Cost Multi-Path routing in IP underlay networks. Its adoption was further accelerated by strong support from networking hardware vendors and integration with major hypervisors. However, VXLAN was designed with simplicity in mind, and as a result, its header format is fixed and lacks native support for extensible metadata. This rigidity limits its ability to adapt to advanced use cases such as service chaining, fine-grained policy enforcement, or telemetry.

NVGRE, or Network Virtualization using Generic Routing Encapsulation, was introduced by Microsoft as part of its Hyper-V ecosystem. It also aimed to overcome VLAN limitations by using GRE for encapsulation and embedding a 24-bit Tenant Network Identifier within the GRE key field. Like VXLAN, NVGRE allows for a large number of isolated virtual networks. However, NVGRE's adoption has been more limited due to its tight coupling with Microsoft technologies and the lack of broad industry support outside the Windows Server environment. Additionally, GRE's lack of a transport layer, such as UDP or TCP, makes it less efficient for load balancing using ECMP in many data center networks. NVGRE does not include a standardized control plane and depends on centralized policy servers for endpoint mapping and forwarding decisions. Its lack of extensibility and minimal hardware acceleration support have limited its relevance in more diverse and programmable network environments.

GENEVE, or Generic Network Virtualization Encapsulation, was developed to address the limitations and fragmentation seen in earlier protocols like VXLAN and NVGRE. GENEVE retains the beneficial aspects of its predecessors, such as a 24-bit Virtual Network Identifier and IP-based tunneling using UDP. However, it introduces a flexible and extensible header format that includes a variable-length options field for carrying metadata. This feature is its most important innovation. The metadata options are encoded using a Type-Length-Value structure, allowing for custom and standardized attributes to be embedded in packets. These can include tenant information, security groups, telemetry data, service chain identifiers, application labels, and more. This extensibility enables a level of programmability and adaptability that neither VXLAN nor NVGRE can achieve without protocol modification or vendor-specific extensions.

The extensibility of GENEVE makes it particularly well suited for integration with software-defined networking architectures and cloud-native platforms. In environments that rely on centralized controllers for traffic steering, policy enforcement, or dynamic service insertion, GENEVE can be used to carry controller-generated context directly within each packet. This eliminates the need for intermediate devices to perform lookups or maintain extensive state tables. By comparison, VXLAN and NVGRE require additional mechanisms or external control planes to achieve similar outcomes, often at the expense of increased complexity and reduced efficiency.

Another major advantage of GENEVE over VXLAN and NVGRE is its ability to support service function chaining in a standardized and scalable way. GENEVE's options field can encode the sequence and parameters of network functions a packet must traverse, allowing each service to inspect and act upon the metadata as needed. VXLAN, lacking this extensible structure, must rely on external orchestration or use proprietary methods to achieve similar results. NVGRE is even more limited in this regard, as its GRE-based encapsulation and lack of metadata support prevent dynamic service chaining without complex workarounds.

From a hardware support perspective, VXLAN enjoys the widest adoption and mature ecosystem. It is natively supported by most modern network switches and NICs, making it easy to offload encapsulation and decapsulation to hardware. NVGRE, by contrast, has limited hardware acceleration options, and support is often restricted to Microsoft-specific environments. GENEVE is newer and has not yet reached the same level of hardware adoption as VXLAN, but this is changing rapidly. With the rise of programmable hardware such as smart NICs and P4-capable switches, support for GENEVE's flexible metadata parsing is becoming more practical. Several vendors are already implementing GENEVE offload features, particularly for common option types, making it increasingly viable in high-performance environments.

In terms of control plane integration, VXLAN has evolved significantly through the introduction of BGP EVPN as a distributed control plane. This development provides VXLAN with a scalable and standardized method of endpoint discovery and route distribution. NVGRE has no equivalent distributed control plane and relies instead on centralized policy servers. GENEVE, while agnostic to control plane mechanisms, is highly compatible with both centralized and distributed models. It can operate effectively with OVN, OpenDaylight, or custom SDN controllers, and its metadata capabilities enhance the control plane's ability to influence packet forwarding directly through in-band signaling.

When comparing these protocols in terms of operational visibility and troubleshooting, GENEVE again stands out. Its ability to carry in-band telemetry, diagnostics, and flow identifiers simplifies network monitoring and performance management. VXLAN requires additional tooling or flow-based inspection to achieve similar visibility, and NVGRE is limited in terms of introspection capabilities. In environments where observability and real-time analytics are critical, GENEVE provides a foundation for richer and more actionable insights.

Ultimately, the choice between GENEVE, VXLAN, and NVGRE depends on the goals and constraints of the environment in which they are deployed. VXLAN is ideal for environments that prioritize broad vendor support, mature tooling, and compatibility with existing infrastructure. NVGRE may still be appropriate in Microsoft-centric data centers where Hyper-V integration and simple overlay models are sufficient. GENEVE is the most forward-looking and adaptable of the three, designed to meet the demands of modern, programmable, and dynamic networks. Its extensibility, metadata capabilities, and alignment with SDN make it a powerful enabler for cloud-native architectures, automated policy enforcement, and intelligent service delivery. As network requirements continue to evolve, GENEVE offers the flexibility and control necessary to support the next generation of virtualized networking.

Overlay Networking in SDN Architectures

The integration of overlay networking into Software-Defined Networking (SDN) architectures represents one of the most transformative developments in modern network design. SDN introduced the idea of decoupling the control plane from the data plane, giving rise to networks that are programmable, centrally managed, and dynamically adaptable. Overlay networking, on the other hand, provided a mechanism to abstract logical network segments from the constraints of physical infrastructure by encapsulating traffic in tunneling protocols such as VXLAN, NVGRE, or GENEVE. When these two paradigms converge, the result is an architecture that delivers unprecedented levels of scalability, flexibility, automation, and operational efficiency. Overlay networks in SDN enable seamless network virtualization and form the foundation for multi-tenant, cloud-native, and hybrid infrastructures.

At its core, overlay networking solves a critical problem: how to build isolated, flexible network topologies that span disparate physical locations without reconfiguring the underlying hardware. In SDN environments, overlays are essential for creating virtual networks that can be provisioned on demand and managed entirely through software. These overlays consist of virtual switches and tunnels that encapsulate traffic between endpoints, allowing the creation of logical Layer 2 and Layer 3 topologies atop a shared Layer 3 physical fabric. This abstraction aligns perfectly with the SDN philosophy of centralized intelligence and distributed forwarding. The SDN controller orchestrates the creation and management of the overlay, while the encapsulation protocols carry traffic with the necessary tenant, application, or service context embedded in the packet headers.

One of the most powerful benefits of using overlay networking within SDN architectures is the ability to support multi-tenancy at scale. By assigning each tenant or application a unique virtual network identifier, the SDN controller ensures that all traffic is properly segmented and that policies are applied consistently. This segmentation is independent of IP addressing or VLAN tagging in the physical network, allowing for overlapping IP spaces and flexible network designs. The encapsulation headers used in overlay protocols carry this segmentation information, which is interpreted by tunnel endpoints to enforce isolation and forwarding behavior. In a well-designed SDN overlay, the logical topology is completely decoupled from the physical network, allowing operators to move, scale, or reconfigure workloads without changing any underlay configurations.

Overlay networking also enhances workload mobility and elasticity, two key tenets of cloud and virtualization platforms. In traditional networks, moving a virtual machine or container from one host to another could require reconfiguring VLANs, updating routing tables, or even causing temporary loss of connectivity. In an SDN-enabled overlay network, the controller is aware of all endpoint locations and can dynamically update tunnel mappings and flow rules to maintain seamless connectivity during workload migration. This capability enables live migration of virtual machines, automated failover, and elastic scaling of applications across hosts, racks, and even data centers without manual intervention or service disruption.

Security is another area where overlay networking in SDN architectures provides significant advantages. Because the SDN controller maintains a centralized view of all traffic flows and tenant contexts, it can enforce security policies at a granular level. Microsegmentation becomes straightforward, with rules applied to individual workloads based on identity, application role, or metadata carried within the overlay header. Network functions such as firewalls, intrusion prevention systems, and deep packet inspection engines can be dynamically inserted into traffic paths based on policy or behavior. These service chains are defined by the controller and encoded in metadata fields, enabling inline inspection and enforcement without requiring changes to the application or physical topology.

The programmability of SDN, combined with the abstraction of overlays, also facilitates automation and integration with orchestration platforms. Infrastructure as Code becomes a reality, where networks are provisioned alongside compute and storage resources through APIs and declarative configurations. Virtual networks, tunnels, and policies are defined in templates or automation scripts, reducing human error and accelerating deployment times. Overlay networks respond to changes in application demands, user behavior, or security posture in real time, as the controller reprograms the data plane to adapt. This dynamic behavior is essential in DevOps-driven environments and supports rapid application delivery and continuous deployment.

Telemetry and observability are enhanced through overlay networking in SDN architectures as well. The SDN controller can monitor flows, tunnel states, and endpoint behavior from a centralized point. Some overlay protocols, like GENEVE, support in-band telemetry, allowing performance data to travel within the same packets as user traffic. This in-band approach enables real-time monitoring of latency, loss, and congestion without requiring dedicated probe traffic. Combined with analytics engines and machine learning models, this data enables predictive operations, anomaly detection, and intelligent troubleshooting, all of which contribute to a more resilient and self-healing network infrastructure.

Hybrid and multi-cloud scenarios are particularly well served by the combination of SDN and overlay networking. Organizations that span multiple data centers or integrate with public cloud platforms can use overlays to create consistent network environments across all locations. The SDN controller manages the connectivity between cloud regions, on-premises infrastructure, and edge sites, using tunnels to maintain secure and seamless communication. Overlays extend the reach of policies and segmentation boundaries, enabling consistent enforcement and compliance even in highly distributed environments. Workloads can move between locations without breaking network dependencies, and global services can be deployed with uniform connectivity and visibility.

The choice of overlay protocol also plays an important role in SDN architectures. VXLAN has broad hardware support and is widely used in enterprise data centers. It is suitable for scenarios where simplicity and interoperability are key. NVGRE, though less common, is still used in some Microsoft-centric environments. GENEVE offers the most flexibility, especially in controller-based SDN architectures, due to its extensible header format and support for custom metadata. Controllers can use GENEVE to carry context-rich information, enabling more intelligent forwarding, policy enforcement, and service chaining. Regardless of the protocol, the SDN controller abstracts the complexity of tunnel management and ensures that the overlay functions as a coherent, policy-driven network.

Overlay networking in SDN architectures is a foundational capability that enables the shift toward fully virtualized, automated, and programmable infrastructure. By decoupling logical networks from physical constraints, supporting dynamic behavior, and integrating deeply with orchestration and security frameworks, overlays make it possible to build networks that are as agile and scalable as the applications they support. As cloud computing, edge services, and hybrid deployments continue to evolve, the role of overlays within SDN will only become more critical, providing the flexibility and control necessary to meet the demands of modern digital ecosystems.

Role of Controllers in Overlay Networks

Controllers are central to the architecture and operation of overlay networks in modern software-defined environments. They function as the brains of the system, abstracting the underlying infrastructure and providing centralized intelligence for configuring, monitoring, and optimizing the overlay fabric. Overlay networks allow multiple virtual networks to coexist over a shared physical infrastructure by encapsulating tenant traffic using tunneling protocols such as VXLAN, NVGRE, or GENEVE. While the encapsulation process provides isolation and flexibility, the complexity of dynamically provisioning and managing large-scale overlays demands a control mechanism that can maintain consistent state and respond to changes quickly and efficiently. This is where controllers play a transformative role.

In traditional networks, control plane functions such as path selection, address resolution, and policy enforcement are distributed across individual network devices. These devices operate autonomously based on static configurations or localized protocols, which often leads to complexity, inefficiencies, and configuration drift. Overlay networks introduce an additional layer of abstraction that must be coordinated across many endpoints. Controllers shift the paradigm by centralizing decision-making. They maintain a global view of the network topology, endpoint locations, tenant policies, and available resources. With this holistic awareness, the controller can determine optimal forwarding paths, assign virtual network identifiers, and enforce isolation boundaries without manual intervention on each device.

The most basic role of a controller in an overlay network is to manage the lifecycle of tunnels and virtual networks. When a tenant or application requests a new network segment, the controller provisions the corresponding identifiers, such as VNIs in VXLAN or TNIs in NVGRE, and establishes the required tunnel endpoints between participating devices. These endpoints may reside in virtual switches on hypervisors, smart NICs, or physical switches supporting overlay protocols. The controller pushes configuration to these endpoints, instructing them on how to encapsulate and decapsulate traffic, how to interpret metadata, and how to forward packets to the appropriate destinations. This process is automated and consistent, reducing provisioning time from hours or days to seconds.

Beyond tunnel provisioning, controllers are responsible for endpoint discovery and mobility. In dynamic environments where virtual machines and containers are constantly moving across hosts, maintaining accurate location information is critical for proper forwarding. The controller keeps track of where each workload resides and updates tunnel mappings accordingly. When a workload moves, the controller immediately updates the forwarding tables in all relevant devices to ensure seamless connectivity. This capability supports live migration, automated scaling, and rapid failure recovery without requiring manual reconfiguration or introducing service disruption.

Policy enforcement is another essential function performed by controllers in overlay networks. Because the controller understands the identity, role, and context of each endpoint, it can apply fine-grained policies that govern communication between workloads. These policies may include access control rules, service chaining directives, quality-of-service parameters, and traffic steering preferences. The controller translates high-level intent into concrete flow rules that are installed on network devices. This approach enables microsegmentation, tenant isolation, and compliance with security frameworks. Since the controller can update policies in real time, network behavior can be adapted dynamically based on threat intelligence, user behavior, or workload changes.

Controllers also enable advanced service chaining within overlay networks. Many applications rely on sequences of network functions such as firewalls, load balancers, intrusion detection systems, or deep packet inspection engines. Rather than relying on static paths or complex configurations, controllers define service chains as logical policies. These policies dictate the order and conditions under which traffic should pass through various services. In protocols like GENEVE, the controller can encode service chain information directly into the packet metadata, allowing each function to process traffic based on its position in the chain. This approach simplifies service orchestration and supports elastic scaling of network functions based on load or demand.

Observability and telemetry are also greatly enhanced by the presence of a centralized controller. Because it maintains a global view of the network and all active flows, the controller is in a unique position to collect, analyze, and act upon performance data. It can correlate metrics across overlay and underlay layers, identify bottlenecks, and make intelligent routing adjustments to optimize throughput and reduce latency. In many implementations, the controller integrates with telemetry systems to ingest flow statistics, packet drops, latency measurements, and other key performance indicators. This data enables proactive management, root cause analysis, and capacity planning, all of which are critical in maintaining service levels in complex environments.

Integration with orchestration platforms is another vital function that controllers serve. In cloud environments, workloads are typically created, scaled, and destroyed through orchestrators like OpenStack, Kubernetes, or VMware vSphere. The controller interfaces with these platforms via APIs, ensuring that network configuration matches the desired state of compute resources. When a new virtual machine or pod is created, the orchestrator informs the controller, which then provisions the necessary network elements, including tunnel endpoints, policies, and routing rules. This tight coupling between compute and network management ensures that application delivery is fast, consistent, and secure.

Security is further enhanced through controller-driven oversight. Because the controller is aware of all endpoints and their communication patterns, it can detect anomalies that may indicate compromised systems or malicious activity. It can also enforce isolation boundaries and prevent unauthorized traffic from traversing virtual networks. With integration into identity and access management systems, the controller can apply policies based on user roles, organizational groups, or compliance tags. This identity-aware networking model adds another layer of protection and ensures that only authorized users and applications can communicate.

In multi-site and hybrid cloud deployments, the role of the controller becomes even more critical. It must coordinate overlay networking across geographically dispersed locations and maintain consistent policy enforcement regardless of where workloads reside. The controller establishes secure tunnels between sites, replicates network and policy state, and manages failover scenarios. This enables seamless workload mobility and disaster recovery strategies while maintaining the same level of performance and security as a single-site deployment.

The evolution of controllers in overlay networks reflects the broader shift toward automation, programmability, and intent-based networking. Controllers enable infrastructure to be abstracted, networks to be treated as code, and services to be delivered in real time. As overlay protocols continue to evolve and support richer metadata and telemetry, the role of the controller will expand even further. It will not only manage configuration and policy but also serve as the central nervous system for intelligent, adaptive, and resilient network infrastructures. Through analytics, machine learning, and closed-loop automation, controllers will make networks increasingly self-optimizing and self-healing, laying the groundwork for the future of autonomous networking.

Overlay and Underlay Network Design

The relationship between overlay and underlay network design is a critical aspect of building scalable, resilient, and efficient modern data center infrastructures. Overlay networks are logical, virtualized topologies that operate on top of the physical infrastructure, while underlay networks consist of the physical devices and routing protocols that move actual packets across the fabric. Understanding the interaction between these two layers is essential for network architects and operators who aim to deploy technologies such as VXLAN, NVGRE, and GENEVE in environments driven by software-defined networking, virtualization, and cloud-native application demands. The success of an overlay deployment is not only dependent on the features of the overlay protocol itself but also heavily influenced by the design, stability, and performance of the underlay.

In an overlay architecture, logical network segments are created independently of the underlying physical topology. These segments are connected through tunneling mechanisms, and traffic between endpoints is encapsulated to maintain isolation and carry metadata necessary for forwarding decisions. Overlay protocols such as VXLAN encapsulate Layer 2 frames within Layer 3 packets, allowing communication across Layer 3 boundaries while preserving tenant isolation. These encapsulated packets are transmitted across the underlay infrastructure, which is typically composed of IP routers, switches, and transport links configured to support high throughput and low latency. The overlay, therefore, depends entirely on the underlay for reliable packet delivery, making the performance and consistency of the underlay network a foundational component of any successful deployment.

One of the most common challenges in overlay and underlay design is achieving alignment between the logical and physical layers without creating unnecessary complexity or performance bottlenecks. Overlay networks allow for flexible and dynamic topologies, but these virtual designs must be supported by an underlay that can handle the traffic patterns generated by encapsulated flows. The underlay must be designed with sufficient capacity, fault tolerance, and path diversity to ensure that tunneled traffic reaches its destination without degradation. Leaf-spine architectures are widely adopted in data centers to address this need, offering predictable latency, equal-cost multi-path (ECMP) routing, and scalable bandwidth. The use of ECMP is particularly important in overlay designs, as it allows multiple encapsulated flows to be distributed across available paths, maximizing throughput and avoiding congestion.

Encapsulation overhead introduced by overlay protocols is another important consideration in underlay network design. Protocols like VXLAN and GENEVE add additional bytes to each packet, including outer IP and UDP headers as well as protocol-specific fields. This increases the overall packet size and can lead to fragmentation if the underlay is not configured with appropriately sized maximum transmission units (MTUs). To prevent fragmentation and maintain performance, the underlay must support jumbo frames that can accommodate the full size of encapsulated packets. Failure to do so results in unnecessary CPU utilization, reduced throughput, and increased packet loss due to fragmentation across intermediate links. Ensuring consistent MTU configuration across the underlay is a crucial step in overlay network readiness.

Another important design principle is ensuring simplicity and predictability in the underlay while allowing complexity to reside in the overlay. The underlay should be treated as a transport layer, providing IP connectivity with minimal intelligence or state. Routing protocols such as OSPF, IS-IS, or BGP are commonly used to maintain underlay connectivity and provide fast convergence in the event of link or node failure. By keeping the underlay simple, operators reduce operational risk, enhance reliability, and make troubleshooting easier. The overlay, on the other hand, can support rich features such as segmentation, security policies, service chaining, and telemetry, all orchestrated by software-defined controllers.

Visibility and monitoring present another layer of complexity in overlay and underlay integration. Network operators must be able to observe both the logical flow of application traffic in the overlay and the physical path that encapsulated packets take through the underlay. Traditional monitoring tools are often limited in their ability to correlate overlay flows with underlay metrics, making it difficult to identify the root cause of performance issues. To address this, modern tools are being developed that provide cross-layer visibility, correlating flow records, latency measurements, and path tracing across both layers. Protocols like in-band network telemetry (INT) and support for flow-based analytics embedded in GENEVE headers allow for more granular observability. Effective overlay and underlay monitoring enables proactive troubleshooting, capacity planning, and service level assurance.

Security is also influenced by the overlay-underlay relationship. While overlays provide logical segmentation and tenant isolation, they must be supported by secure underlay designs that prevent unauthorized access, sniffing of encapsulated traffic, or injection of rogue packets. Encryption between tunnel endpoints, access control lists on underlay devices, and separation of management and data planes are important considerations. Overlay metadata can also be used to apply dynamic security policies at the edges of the network. However, if the underlay is compromised, encapsulated traffic is vulnerable to interception or tampering. For this reason, underlay hardening, including physical security and protocol-level protections, remains a critical part of any overlay-enabled environment.

The coordination between overlay and underlay design extends into automation and orchestration. Many modern infrastructures rely on automation platforms to manage both network layers, ensuring that configurations are synchronized and responsive to changes in the environment. When a new virtual machine is provisioned, automation tools configure overlay policies while also validating underlay reachability and tunnel endpoint availability. This end-to-end orchestration ensures that the overlay can be deployed without manual intervention and that performance, security, and compliance standards are maintained. Tools that unify configuration and policy management across overlay and underlay layers reduce operational complexity and support faster time to service delivery.

Resiliency and failover mechanisms must also be considered across both network layers. The underlay must support rapid link and node failover using techniques like fast reroute and BFD (Bidirectional Forwarding Detection). The overlay must be designed to detect changes in endpoint reachability and adjust tunnel paths or routing entries accordingly. In controller-based environments, the SDN controller plays a key role in reconciling changes in the underlay and adjusting overlay configurations to ensure service continuity. Designing overlays that can recover from underlay disruptions without affecting application performance is a key goal of resilient network architecture.

Overlay and underlay network design must be approached as a unified architectural exercise. While overlays provide the abstraction necessary to support scalable, flexible, and tenant-aware networks, the physical underlay determines the reliability, efficiency, and overall performance of the system. By aligning the capabilities of the underlay with the demands of the overlay, architects can build infrastructures that are not only agile and programmable but also robust and operationally sound. This alignment supports the goals of cloud computing, microservices, and digital transformation, ensuring that the network can scale and adapt as fast as the applications it is designed to support.

Interoperability Between Overlay Protocols

The evolution of overlay networking protocols such as VXLAN, NVGRE, and GENEVE has brought significant advancements in how data centers and cloud networks manage segmentation, scalability, and workload mobility. These protocols enable the creation of logical network topologies independent of the physical infrastructure, allowing organizations to scale networks quickly and support multi-tenancy, isolation, and dynamic service insertion. However, as networks become increasingly heterogeneous and complex, the question of interoperability between different overlay protocols becomes more pressing. It is not uncommon to find environments where different technologies coexist due to vendor preferences, legacy infrastructure, or varied deployment timelines. In such environments, ensuring interoperability across overlay protocols becomes essential to maintaining unified connectivity, consistent policy enforcement, and efficient operational workflows.

Interoperability challenges arise primarily because each overlay protocol was designed independently with unique encapsulation formats, control plane mechanisms, and operational goals. VXLAN encapsulates Ethernet frames using a UDP-based format and introduces a 24-bit VXLAN Network Identifier. It is widely adopted and supported across multiple hardware and software platforms, making it the de facto standard in many enterprise networks. NVGRE, introduced by Microsoft, uses GRE for encapsulation and also includes a 24-bit tenant network identifier in the GRE key field. Its use has been more limited and typically confined to Microsoft-centric environments such as Hyper-V and System Center. GENEVE, the most recent of the three, builds upon lessons learned from its predecessors and adds a flexible metadata structure to support a wide range of use cases. It is highly extensible and designed with software-defined networking and programmability in mind.

These differences in header structure and design philosophy make native interoperability between protocols complex. A VXLAN endpoint does not understand a GENEVE header, nor can it interpret the encapsulated metadata. Similarly, an NVGRE tunnel endpoint cannot process VXLAN packets. Without a translation mechanism or interworking function, endpoints configured for one protocol are essentially blind to traffic originating from a different overlay domain. This lack of native compatibility poses significant challenges when merging networks after acquisitions, integrating services from different vendors, or transitioning from one overlay technology to another.

To address these challenges, the industry has developed a range of techniques for enabling interoperability between overlay protocols. One of the most common approaches is the use of gateway devices or software components that serve as translation points between overlay domains. These gateways are capable of decapsulating traffic from one overlay protocol, interpreting its headers and metadata, and re-encapsulating it in another format. For example, a gateway can receive a VXLAN-encapsulated packet, extract the original Ethernet frame, and repackage it using GENEVE for transmission into another domain. This translation process involves not only rewriting encapsulation headers but also translating or preserving network identifiers, policy markers, and service-related metadata to maintain functionality and security across the domains.

Such translation requires careful handling of metadata, especially when dealing with protocols like GENEVE that support extensive option fields. Some metadata may have no direct equivalent in the target protocol, necessitating the use of mapping tables or policy engines to preserve semantics. In some cases, metadata may be discarded if it is not supported by the destination protocol, which could affect service chaining, telemetry, or security enforcement. To minimize loss of functionality, gateways often implement policy negotiation or context preservation features to replicate the original intent of the overlay-specific metadata in a form understandable to the receiving domain.

Control plane interoperability is another significant challenge in environments using different overlay protocols. Each protocol may rely on a different mechanism for endpoint discovery, MAC learning, and route distribution. VXLAN with EVPN uses BGP as a control plane, enabling distributed learning of MAC and IP address bindings. NVGRE traditionally relies on centralized policy servers for address mapping, while GENEVE is typically used in SDN environments with controllers that manage policy and endpoint state. Bridging these control planes requires integration at the orchestration or controller layer, where a unified platform maintains a global view of endpoints across all domains and programs translation devices accordingly. Some SDN controllers and orchestration platforms are capable of managing mixed-overlay environments, acting as a centralized brain that harmonizes policies, mappings, and flow rules across the fabric.

Another approach to promoting interoperability is the adoption of standardized interfaces and APIs. By exposing network services through standardized RESTful APIs, overlay domains can interoperate at the service layer, even if they use different encapsulation methods at the transport layer. For example, orchestration tools can provision networks, assign security policies, and configure service chains across VXLAN and GENEVE domains through a single API framework. This abstraction decouples the service intent from the underlying protocol and enables cross-domain consistency. It also supports gradual migration from one overlay technology to another, allowing legacy workloads to operate alongside newer deployments without requiring full conversion.

In environments where full protocol translation is impractical, interoperability can also be achieved through policy-based routing and segmentation. Traffic destined for workloads in a different overlay domain can be directed to a specific interconnection point where traffic policies are applied, and segmentation is preserved through VLAN tags, IP subnets, or virtual routing instances. While this method does not offer the same level of integration as protocol translation, it allows for controlled communication between overlay domains while maintaining isolation and security. It is especially useful in staged migration scenarios or in service provider networks where customers operate using different overlay technologies.

Performance and operational considerations must also be taken into account when implementing interoperability between overlay protocols. The translation process adds latency and may become a bottleneck if not properly scaled. Gateways must be designed to handle high throughput and provide fault tolerance to ensure that inter-domain communication is resilient. Monitoring and visibility tools must be able to correlate flows across domains and protocols, requiring deep packet inspection or metadata tagging to track flows end to end. Operators must invest in unified observability platforms that span the entire overlay landscape, providing insights into tunnel health, policy enforcement, and application performance.

Interoperability between overlay protocols reflects the broader trend of heterogeneity in network environments. Organizations are unlikely to standardize on a single vendor or technology across all infrastructure layers, making protocol coexistence a practical reality. By leveraging translation gateways, control plane integration, service-level abstraction, and policy-driven segmentation, network architects can build overlay fabrics that operate seamlessly across protocol boundaries. This flexibility supports business agility, enables cloud interconnectivity, and provides a path for gradual modernization of legacy networks while preserving operational consistency and security across the entire environment.

Network Virtualization and Security

Network virtualization has transformed how modern infrastructures are designed, operated, and secured. It allows multiple isolated logical networks to coexist over a shared physical infrastructure, enabling multi-tenancy, efficient resource utilization, and rapid provisioning of services. As organizations move toward more dynamic and scalable environments, particularly in cloud computing and software-defined data centers, network virtualization has become a foundational technology. However, with this increased abstraction and flexibility comes the challenge of maintaining robust and consistent security across a virtualized network landscape. Security in virtualized networks must address not only traditional threats but also new risks introduced by the programmability, mobility, and multi-tenancy inherent in these architectures.

At the core of network virtualization is the decoupling of the logical network topology from the underlying physical infrastructure. This abstraction enables the creation of virtual switches, routers, firewalls, and other network functions that exist entirely in software. Virtual networks can span multiple physical hosts and even data centers, with traffic tunneled using overlay protocols such as VXLAN, NVGRE, or GENEVE. These overlays carry not only the data payload but also metadata that defines the context of each flow, such as tenant identification, quality of service, or security policy requirements. While this model improves agility and scalability, it also increases the attack surface and creates new challenges for visibility and control.

One of the primary security concerns in virtualized networks is ensuring tenant isolation. In multi-tenant environments, each tenant must be guaranteed that their traffic is logically and cryptographically separated from that of others. Overlay protocols help achieve this by using unique network identifiers, such as VXLAN VNIs or GENEVE TNIs, that encapsulate tenant traffic within dedicated tunnels. These identifiers enforce segmentation at the data plane level, ensuring that traffic cannot be inadvertently or maliciously routed across boundaries. However, this logical isolation is only effective if enforced consistently across all virtual switches, hypervisors, and physical network elements. Any misconfiguration or software vulnerability could lead to cross-tenant leakage or unauthorized access, undermining the fundamental premise of network virtualization.

Another major area of concern is visibility and monitoring. In traditional physical networks, traffic flows are easier to inspect using hardware taps or span ports. In virtualized environments, traffic is often encapsulated, distributed across hosts, and processed in software. This makes it harder to apply conventional intrusion detection or deep packet inspection techniques. Security tools must be capable of understanding and parsing overlay headers, correlating metadata with security policies, and operating at both the virtual and physical layers. GENEVE, for example, allows security metadata to be embedded within the encapsulation header, offering a mechanism for in-band security tagging. This can improve the ability of firewalls and monitoring tools to apply context-aware filtering, but only if those tools are capable of interpreting the metadata correctly.

Microsegmentation has emerged as one of the most effective security strategies in network virtualization. It involves creating fine-grained security zones around individual workloads, allowing only explicitly authorized traffic between them. Unlike traditional perimeter-based models, microsegmentation enforces policies at the workload level, regardless of network topology or IP addressing. This is particularly important in dynamic environments where workloads move frequently and may span multiple subnets or hosts. SDN controllers and policy engines enforce microsegmentation rules by programming virtual switches with flow-based policies. These rules can be based on a variety of attributes, including IP addresses, ports, protocols, user identity, and application role. The result is a highly granular security model that reduces the attack surface and limits lateral movement in the event of a breach.

Encryption is another critical component of securing virtualized networks. Overlay protocols can be combined with transport-layer encryption mechanisms such as IPsec or TLS to ensure that traffic remains confidential and tamper-proof as it traverses the physical infrastructure. This is particularly important in hybrid cloud or multi-site deployments where data may cross untrusted or public networks. Some implementations also support MACsec at the link layer to secure traffic between adjacent devices. Encryption not only protects data in transit but also provides a foundation for trust and authentication between tunnel endpoints. Ensuring that keys are managed securely and that encryption overhead does not impact performance are essential considerations in deploying encrypted overlays.

Policy consistency and automation are vital to maintaining security at scale. In virtualized environments, manual configuration is not only error-prone but also incompatible with the pace of change. Security policies must be defined centrally and applied automatically across all relevant network elements. SDN controllers, cloud management platforms, and orchestration tools play a key role in translating high-level intent into enforceable policies. When a new workload is deployed, the platform must automatically assign it to the correct security zone, apply access control rules, and configure any necessary monitoring or logging. This automation reduces human error, accelerates service delivery, and ensures that security is not an afterthought but an integral part of the provisioning process.

Threat detection and response in virtualized networks require a new approach as well. Because traffic patterns and endpoints are more dynamic, traditional signature-based methods may not be sufficient. Behavioral analytics, machine learning, and flow-based anomaly detection are increasingly being used to identify suspicious activity. For example, if a workload begins communicating with previously unseen destinations or exhibits a sudden increase in traffic volume, the system can flag the behavior for further investigation or take automated action. Integrating these detection capabilities with policy engines and SDN controllers allows for rapid containment of threats, such as quarantining affected workloads or redirecting traffic for further inspection.

Compliance and auditability are additional concerns in virtualized networks. Regulations such as GDPR, HIPAA, and PCI-DSS require organizations to demonstrate that appropriate security controls are in place and that sensitive data is protected. Virtual networks must provide mechanisms for logging, auditing, and reporting that span both the overlay and underlay layers. Security events must be correlated with network events, and all policy changes must be traceable to an authorized user or system. Tools that integrate with SIEM platforms and provide a unified view of virtual and physical security posture are essential for meeting compliance requirements and maintaining operational transparency.

As organizations continue to adopt hybrid and multi-cloud strategies, the ability to extend network virtualization and its associated security controls across environments becomes essential. A consistent security model must be maintained across private data centers, public clouds, and edge locations. This requires federation of policy frameworks, consistent use of overlay protocols, and integration of identity and access management systems across domains. Only with a unified security approach can organizations ensure that workloads remain protected regardless of where they run or how they connect.

Network virtualization offers powerful capabilities for building agile, scalable, and efficient infrastructure. However, these benefits must be matched with equally sophisticated security strategies that account for the unique characteristics of virtualized networks. By leveraging microsegmentation, encryption, centralized policy management, automated provisioning, and advanced analytics, organizations can create secure virtual networks that meet the demands of modern applications and regulatory frameworks. Security must be embedded into every layer of the virtual network architecture, not as a reactive measure, but as a proactive design principle that supports agility without compromising protection.

Overlay Networking in Kubernetes

Overlay networking plays a critical role in Kubernetes environments, where highly dynamic, distributed, and containerized workloads demand a scalable, flexible, and isolated network infrastructure. Kubernetes abstracts application deployment and management through containers and orchestrates them across clusters of hosts. These clusters can span multiple nodes, availability zones, or even data centers. As applications are decomposed into microservices that may run across many pods and hosts, Kubernetes requires a robust networking model to ensure reliable communication among services regardless of their physical location. Overlay networking becomes essential in solving the inherent challenges of container communication, multi-tenancy, network isolation, and mobility that arise in Kubernetes-based platforms.

In Kubernetes, every pod receives its own IP address, and the platform mandates a flat network model where all pods can communicate with each other directly without NAT. This requirement is deceptively simple in principle but becomes highly complex in large-scale deployments. Physical networks are typically segmented by VLANs or routing domains, and not all hosts in a cluster are on the same subnet. This is where overlay networks come in. They create a virtual Layer 2 or Layer 3 network that spans across all nodes in the cluster, regardless of their actual physical connectivity. Overlay protocols encapsulate packets within other packets, allowing pod-to-pod communication to occur over the physical network without requiring changes to the underlay topology or IP schema.

Several popular Container Network Interface (CNI) plugins implement overlay networking to satisfy Kubernetes' networking requirements. Examples include Flannel, Calico, Weave, and Cilium. Each of these plugins offers a different approach to building the overlay, with trade-offs in performance, complexity, and features. Flannel, for instance, is one of the simplest CNI plugins and supports multiple backend mechanisms for creating overlays, including VXLAN. In VXLAN mode, Flannel encapsulates pod traffic into UDP packets and routes them between nodes over a VXLAN tunnel. Each node maintains a mapping of pod IP addresses to host IP addresses, enabling it to determine how to reach any other pod in the cluster by encapsulating the traffic and forwarding it through the tunnel.

Weave uses a mesh-based overlay where each node establishes encrypted tunnels with every other node, creating a full-mesh topology that provides direct paths between nodes. This approach is well-suited for smaller clusters or those with more static topologies but may not scale efficiently to thousands of nodes due to tunnel management overhead. Calico originally relied on BGP-based routing rather than overlays but now also supports VXLAN and IP-in-IP overlays to provide flexible options for different environments. Cilium introduces an advanced model using eBPF for data plane processing and supports both native routing and tunneling mechanisms, including GENEVE, to build overlay networks that are aware of application and service-layer context.

Overlay networking in Kubernetes does more than just solve routing problems; it also enables critical security, observability, and scalability features. Network policies in Kubernetes allow administrators to define rules that govern how pods can communicate with each other and with external systems. Overlay networks support the enforcement of these policies by providing logical segmentation and enabling distributed enforcement at the pod level. When combined with security metadata or labels, policies can be enforced dynamically, even as pods are created, destroyed, or moved across the cluster. This form of microsegmentation ensures that only authorized communication paths are permitted, reducing the risk of lateral movement by attackers and supporting compliance with security standards.

Scalability is another area where overlay networking supports Kubernetes' operational model. In large clusters, pods are frequently created and destroyed based on workload demand, leading to a highly dynamic IP address space. Overlay networks abstract this dynamism by providing consistent routing regardless of changes in the underlying infrastructure. Tunneling protocols handle the encapsulation transparently, allowing services to continue functioning even as endpoints change. This abstraction is particularly valuable in multi-tenant Kubernetes environments where multiple teams or applications share the same physical infrastructure but require isolation from one another. Each tenant's workloads can be deployed into their own namespace with overlay-backed policies ensuring that their traffic remains segregated.

Overlay networks also play a role in cross-cluster and hybrid cloud Kubernetes deployments. As organizations seek to federate multiple clusters or extend their Kubernetes workloads across cloud providers and on-premises data centers, overlay networking provides a consistent layer of connectivity. Tunnels can be established between clusters, allowing services to discover and communicate with each other as if they were on the same logical network. This enables use cases such as disaster recovery, global load balancing, and regional redundancy, all while maintaining secure and reliable network communication. GENEVE, with its extensible metadata model, is particularly well-suited for such scenarios, allowing identity, policy, and telemetry information to be carried alongside traffic across clusters.

Observability is greatly enhanced by the programmability of overlay networks in Kubernetes. With the integration of tools such as Prometheus, Grafana, and OpenTelemetry, administrators can monitor not only the performance of services but also the state of the overlay itself. Metrics related to tunnel health, packet drops, latency, and flow counts can be collected and analyzed to detect anomalies, optimize routing, and plan capacity. In advanced deployments, service meshes such as Istio or Linkerd further extend the overlay model by introducing sidecars that intercept and manage traffic between pods, adding capabilities such as encryption, retries, load balancing, and detailed telemetry without requiring changes to the applications themselves.

Performance remains a critical consideration when implementing overlay networking in Kubernetes. Encapsulation introduces overhead, both in terms of bandwidth and CPU usage. Each packet must be encapsulated and decapsulated at tunnel endpoints, and the additional headers increase packet size. In high-throughput environments, this can lead to bottlenecks unless mitigated by hardware offloading or efficient software processing such as eBPF. Smart NICs that support VXLAN or GENEVE offloading can significantly improve performance by handling encapsulation tasks in hardware. Similarly, using kernel bypass techniques or user-space networking frameworks allows CNI plugins to achieve high performance without sacrificing flexibility or observability.

Overlay networking in Kubernetes is not simply a workaround for networking challenges. It is a foundational capability that enables the platform to support the agility, scale, and isolation that modern applications demand. It abstracts the complexity of the physical network, provides secure and consistent connectivity across dynamic environments, and integrates with policy, monitoring, and orchestration layers to deliver a comprehensive networking solution. As Kubernetes continues to evolve as the standard for container orchestration across enterprises and cloud providers, overlay networking will remain a key enabler of its success, ensuring that applications can communicate securely, perform reliably, and scale efficiently in any environment.

Integration with Network Function Virtualization

The integration of overlay networking with Network Function Virtualization (NFV) represents a powerful convergence of two transformative technologies in modern networking. NFV is a framework that decouples network functions such as firewalls, load balancers, intrusion detection systems, and routers from proprietary hardware appliances and allows them to run as virtualized software instances on standard servers. Overlay networking, by abstracting logical network topologies from the physical infrastructure through encapsulation techniques, provides the flexibility and segmentation necessary to dynamically connect and manage these virtualized functions. Together, these technologies enable highly programmable, scalable, and cost-effective network architectures suitable for service providers, enterprises, and cloud platforms.

One of the primary goals of NFV is to bring agility to network service deployment. Traditionally, network services were delivered using purpose-built hardware appliances that were expensive to scale and slow to provision. In contrast, NFV allows these services to be deployed on-demand as virtual network functions, or VNFs, which can be instantiated, moved, or scaled in response to traffic patterns or service requirements. However, VNFs must be connected in specific sequences, often forming service chains where traffic must pass through multiple functions before reaching its destination. Overlay networks provide the foundation for creating these service chains by enabling flexible and isolated traffic paths that can be programmed independently of the physical network.

Encapsulation protocols such as VXLAN, NVGRE, and GENEVE are instrumental in enabling this integration. These protocols allow for the transport of encapsulated packets across a shared underlay network, maintaining logical separation between tenants, services, or traffic classes. In NFV environments, this is critical because multiple service chains often operate concurrently, each with its own set of network functions and policies. By tagging traffic with virtual network identifiers and additional metadata, overlays ensure that packets follow the correct service chain and maintain context as they pass through each VNF. This capability is particularly advanced in GENEVE, which supports extensible metadata fields that can carry service chain identifiers, policy tags, or telemetry data.

The orchestration layer plays a crucial role in managing the integration of overlays with NFV. In NFV architectures, the Management and Orchestration (MANO) framework is responsible for lifecycle management of VNFs, including provisioning, scaling, monitoring, and healing. The MANO interacts with SDN controllers and overlay network managers to ensure that each VNF is connected to the appropriate virtual networks. When a new service chain is defined, the orchestration platform not only launches the VNFs but also programs the overlay tunnels, installs the necessary flow rules, and ensures that the encapsulation headers carry the correct context. This tight integration between network and compute orchestration is essential for automating the deployment of complex services.

Performance is a key consideration in the integration of overlay networks with NFV. VNFs often handle high-throughput traffic and may be sensitive to latency or jitter. Encapsulation introduces additional headers and processing overhead, which can impact performance if not properly managed. To address this, modern data center architectures often employ techniques such as hardware offload, Data Plane Development Kit (DPDK) acceleration, and SmartNICs. These technologies enable VNFs to process packets at near line rate, while the network interface handles encapsulation and decapsulation in hardware. This offloading is particularly beneficial in scenarios where GENEVE or VXLAN overlays are used, as the complexity of handling metadata and tunneling can otherwise consume significant CPU resources.

Security is another critical area where overlay networking enhances NFV deployments. Overlay protocols allow for the creation of isolated virtual networks, ensuring that traffic between different tenants or service chains remains segregated. This isolation is enforced at the virtual switch level and supported by metadata that can indicate trust levels, roles, or security policies. Overlay networks can also support encryption, ensuring that traffic between VNFs is protected even if it traverses insecure or shared underlay infrastructure. Furthermore, security functions themselves can be implemented as VNFs, and the overlay enables dynamic insertion of these services into traffic paths. For example, if a particular flow is deemed suspicious, it can be redirected through a deep packet inspection VNF without affecting other traffic.

Visibility and monitoring are essential for ensuring the correct operation of NFV environments. Overlay networks provide mechanisms for embedding telemetry into encapsulated packets, which can then be analyzed by monitoring tools to provide insight into flow behavior, service performance, and fault detection. GENEVE's extensible option fields are particularly suited for this use case, allowing performance metrics, timestamps, or service chain states to be carried within the data plane. This embedded telemetry enables real-time observability and supports closed-loop automation, where orchestration systems can respond dynamically to detected issues by scaling resources, rerouting traffic, or reconfiguring service chains.

Multi-tenancy is a common requirement in NFV, particularly in service provider environments where multiple customers or services must coexist on the same physical infrastructure. Overlay networks are fundamental to supporting this model, as they enable the creation of logically isolated network slices that are managed independently. Each tenant can have its own set of VNFs, address space, and policies, and overlay identifiers ensure that their traffic remains separate. This not only improves security and compliance but also simplifies operations, as network resources can be assigned and managed on a per-tenant basis without affecting others.

The integration of overlay networking with NFV also supports advanced use cases such as network slicing, 5G service delivery, and edge computing. In these scenarios, highly specialized service chains must be deployed close to users or devices, often across geographically distributed locations. Overlay networks allow these services to be instantiated wherever needed and connected through dynamically established tunnels. The flexibility of overlay protocols enables traffic to be steered based on user context, service type, or application requirements, ensuring optimal performance and user experience.

As the networking industry continues to evolve, the integration between overlay networking and NFV will only become deeper and more sophisticated. New standards, such as service interface descriptors and enhanced service function chaining mechanisms, will improve interoperability and automation. Controllers and orchestration platforms will gain more intelligence, enabling them to make real-time decisions based on network conditions, service demands, and policy constraints. Overlay protocols will continue to evolve to support richer metadata, tighter integration with hardware acceleration, and seamless interoperability across domains.

By combining the flexibility of virtualized functions with the programmability and scalability of overlay networks, organizations can build networks that are not only cost-effective and agile but also capable of supporting the diverse and dynamic demands of modern digital services. The ability to instantiate, connect, secure, and monitor network functions entirely in software represents a profound shift in how networks are designed and operated. Overlay networking is not just an enabler for NFV—it is a foundational pillar that supports its full potential in transforming the network into a dynamic, responsive, and intelligent platform.

Overlay Networking in Public Cloud Environments

Overlay networking has become a critical architectural component in public cloud environments, enabling scalable, flexible, and isolated communication across vast multi-tenant infrastructures. As enterprises increasingly migrate workloads to public clouds such as Amazon Web Services, Microsoft Azure, and Google Cloud Platform, the importance of robust network virtualization becomes apparent. Public clouds are built to support millions of concurrent users, applications, and services, all sharing a common physical infrastructure. Overlay networks allow these diverse tenants to operate securely and independently by abstracting the underlying hardware and providing logically segmented virtual networks tailored to each customer's needs. This abstraction, achieved through tunneling protocols and software-defined networking mechanisms, facilitates not only isolation and scalability but also seamless workload mobility, automation, and compliance.

In public cloud environments, overlay networks function by encapsulating tenant traffic in virtual tunnels that span multiple physical hosts, availability zones, or even global regions. These tunnels carry packets from one virtual machine, container, or function to another without requiring those workloads to be aware of the physical layout of the infrastructure. Encapsulation protocols such as VXLAN and GENEVE are commonly used to implement these tunnels, embedding metadata such as tenant identifiers, routing information, and policy tags within the packet headers. The cloud provider's underlying infrastructure is responsible for routing the encapsulated traffic to its destination, where it is decapsulated and delivered to the appropriate virtual endpoint. This approach supports highly elastic and programmable network topologies that can evolve dynamically with application demands.

One of the primary benefits of overlay networking in public clouds is multi-tenancy. Every customer in a public cloud environment expects to operate within an isolated virtual space where their resources are secure and not visible or accessible to other tenants. Overlay networks enforce this isolation by using unique virtual network identifiers and tunneling mechanisms that prevent cross-tenant communication unless explicitly allowed. These logical boundaries extend to IP addressing, routing domains, and access control policies, allowing each tenant to define and manage their own network topologies, subnets, firewalls, and routing tables. From the customer's perspective, this environment behaves like a dedicated private network, even though the underlying infrastructure is shared.

Scalability is another key advantage of overlay networking in the public cloud. Traditional data center networks are constrained by VLAN limits and rigid routing architectures that become difficult to manage at large scale. Overlay networks eliminate these constraints by supporting millions of isolated virtual networks across a single underlay. This scalability is essential for hyperscale cloud providers who must support vast numbers of customers and workloads, each with unique networking requirements. Overlay identifiers such as VXLAN's 24-bit VNI field or GENEVE's extensible metadata structures enable this scale by providing a massive address space for segmenting traffic and associating it with specific tenants, services, or applications.

Overlay networking also enables seamless workload mobility within and across cloud regions. Cloud-native applications often rely on microservices and containerized architectures, which require frequent deployment, scaling, and migration of services across zones or clusters. Overlay tunnels abstract the physical location of services, ensuring that communication paths remain intact even as endpoints move. This abstraction simplifies high availability, disaster recovery, and elastic scaling strategies by decoupling the logical connectivity from the physical topology. Overlay networks, orchestrated by cloud control planes, automatically update mappings and tunnel endpoints to reflect changes in workload placement, maintaining reliable and consistent connectivity.

Security in public cloud overlay networks is deeply integrated into the fabric of the environment. Cloud providers implement granular access controls, security groups, and network policies that govern which resources can communicate over the overlay. These controls are enforced at the hypervisor or virtual switch level, ensuring that unauthorized traffic is dropped before it can traverse the network. Many cloud platforms also offer microsegmentation features that allow customers to define fine-grained rules based on application identity, tags, or security groups. These policies are implemented in distributed firewalls or virtualized enforcement points that operate within the overlay, providing east-west security within virtual networks. Additionally, the metadata capabilities of protocols like GENEVE allow security context to be embedded directly into packets, enabling intelligent inspection and enforcement by security appliances or cloud-native services.

Observability is enhanced through overlay networking by enabling comprehensive monitoring of traffic flows, tunnel performance, and application connectivity. Public cloud providers offer native tools for capturing flow logs, metrics, and telemetry data that can be correlated with application behavior and security events. These tools provide visibility into both underlay and overlay performance, helping administrators diagnose issues, identify bottlenecks, and enforce compliance. In some cases, telemetry is embedded directly into overlay headers, allowing in-band collection of performance data without additional instrumentation. This real-time insight is crucial for managing distributed cloud environments where visibility into each layer of the network is necessary for maintaining service levels and detecting anomalies.

Integration with orchestration and automation platforms is another major benefit of overlay networking in public clouds. Cloud providers expose APIs and infrastructure-as-code interfaces that allow customers to define, provision, and manage virtual networks alongside compute and storage resources. When a new application is deployed, the network is automatically configured to support its requirements, including IP addressing, routing, firewall rules, and security policies. These configurations are applied dynamically across the overlay, enabling rapid deployment and reducing the potential for misconfiguration. Automation also facilitates continuous integration and deployment pipelines, where changes to application code and infrastructure can be tested and promoted in an isolated and controlled network environment.

Hybrid and multi-cloud deployments further underscore the importance of overlay networking in public cloud environments. Enterprises often distribute their workloads across on-premises data centers and multiple public cloud platforms. Overlay networks provide the foundation for consistent networking and security policies across these environments. By establishing encrypted tunnels between environments and using overlay identifiers to segment traffic, organizations can create unified virtual networks that span disparate infrastructures. This capability supports use cases such as burst-to-cloud, backup and disaster recovery, and global application delivery, all while maintaining consistent control and visibility.

Overlay networking in public cloud environments is not only a technical solution but also a strategic enabler for digital transformation. It allows businesses to move faster, operate more securely, and scale more efficiently by abstracting the complexity of physical networking. As applications become more distributed, data becomes more dynamic, and users more global, overlay networks will continue to be the backbone of cloud-native connectivity. They empower organizations to build infrastructure that is not bound by traditional limitations, supporting innovation and agility in a world where change is constant and speed is essential. Overlay networking ensures that regardless of how infrastructure evolves beneath, applications and services remain connected, protected, and performant.

BGP EVPN as a Control Plane

BGP EVPN has emerged as a powerful and scalable control plane for modern overlay networks, offering a standardized and dynamic solution to manage network virtualization and tenant isolation in data centers and cloud environments. It provides a mechanism for exchanging Layer 2 and Layer 3 reachability information using BGP, the widely adopted interdomain routing protocol. BGP EVPN enables dynamic learning of MAC and IP address mappings across the network fabric, eliminating the need for traditional flood-and-learn mechanisms that are commonly associated with earlier overlay implementations such as VXLAN without a control plane. As organizations build more complex and multi-tenant infrastructures, BGP EVPN becomes an essential tool for achieving operational simplicity, efficiency, and scalability.

At its core, BGP EVPN serves as the control plane component in overlay networks where encapsulation protocols such as VXLAN or GENEVE are used to carry tenant traffic across IP fabrics. Traditionally, Ethernet VPNs required extensive broadcast domains and relied on data plane learning to build MAC address tables at each switch. This model did not scale well in large networks and introduced unnecessary broadcast traffic. BGP EVPN replaces these inefficient mechanisms with a model where endpoint reachability information is advertised through BGP updates. Each switch or router participating in the EVPN fabric becomes a BGP speaker, advertising and receiving information about the MAC and IP addresses associated with the endpoints it serves. This information includes the associated VXLAN Network Identifier or other overlay-specific tags, allowing remote switches to build accurate and timely forwarding tables without relying on broadcast frames.

BGP EVPN supports multiple route types that serve different functions within the overlay network. For example, Type 2 routes are used to advertise MAC addresses along with their associated IP addresses, enabling integrated Layer 2 and Layer 3 reachability. Type 3 routes are used for inclusive multicast Ethernet tagging, which helps in replicating broadcast, unknown unicast, and multicast traffic across VXLAN tunnels. Type 5 routes carry IP prefix information, enabling more advanced routing scenarios where entire subnets, rather than individual IP addresses, are advertised. The richness of these route types allows BGP EVPN to support a variety of network topologies and services, from simple Layer 2 extensions to full multi-tenant Layer 3 routing with route leaking and policy control.

One of the most significant advantages of BGP EVPN is its ability to support multi-homing and redundancy through the concept of Ethernet Segment Identifiers (ESIs). In a traditional network, multi-homing can create challenges such as MAC address flapping and inconsistent forwarding behavior. BGP EVPN addresses these issues with an active-active model that supports all-active and single-active multi-homing. By assigning a common ESI to multiple links connecting to the same host or tenant, BGP EVPN ensures that traffic is distributed efficiently and failover is seamless. It uses mechanisms like Designated Forwarder election and MAC mobility to maintain consistent state across the fabric even in the face of link or node failures.

The integration of BGP EVPN with VXLAN enables a fully dynamic and scalable network virtualization solution. VXLAN, as an encapsulation protocol, defines how Layer 2 frames are transported over Layer 3 networks, but it does not define how MAC address learning is performed. In the absence of a control plane, VXLAN relies on flood-and-learn behavior that generates excessive traffic and limits scalability. BGP EVPN fills this gap by providing the intelligence needed to advertise MAC and IP mappings without requiring broadcast frames. This control plane capability is especially critical in environments with high mobility, such as cloud data centers, where virtual machines or containers frequently move between hosts and need their network state to follow them.

Another key benefit of BGP EVPN is its vendor-neutral and standards-based nature. Unlike proprietary control plane solutions, BGP EVPN is defined by multiple IETF RFCs and is supported by a wide range of hardware and software platforms. This interoperability allows organizations to build heterogeneous networks with equipment from different vendors while maintaining consistent behavior and feature support. Furthermore, since BGP is a mature and extensible protocol, network operators are already familiar with its operational model, route policies, and troubleshooting tools. This familiarity reduces the learning curve and operational complexity associated with deploying EVPN-based fabrics.

The use of BGP EVPN also facilitates centralized policy enforcement and route filtering. BGP's policy framework enables administrators to define route maps, prefix lists, and community attributes that control which MAC or IP routes are accepted, preferred, or rejected. This granularity allows for sophisticated traffic engineering and segmentation within the overlay network. For example, operators can control which tenants can communicate across virtual networks, implement route reflection for scaling control plane distribution, and apply traffic shaping or security policies based on route attributes. These capabilities are particularly useful in multi-tenant environments where strict isolation and access control are required.

Scalability is a critical consideration in any control plane design, and BGP EVPN addresses this need through its distributed and hierarchical architecture. It can support thousands of tenants, endpoints, and routes without centralized bottlenecks. The use of route reflectors and BGP communities allows for large-scale deployments that maintain high availability and fast convergence. BGP's incremental update model ensures that only changes are propagated across the network, minimizing control plane churn and reducing the overhead associated with network events. In disaster recovery scenarios or during maintenance events, BGP EVPN's rapid convergence and stability help maintain application uptime and user experience.

The adoption of BGP EVPN is not limited to data center environments. It is increasingly being used in campus, service provider, and multi-cloud networks where consistent policy and mobility are required across diverse locations. Its integration with SDN controllers, automation platforms, and telemetry systems further enhances its value by enabling end-to-end programmability and visibility. Network engineers can use APIs to configure BGP EVPN services, retrieve route data, and respond to operational events with automated workflows. This level of integration supports intent-based networking and aligns with the broader shift toward infrastructure as code and DevOps-driven network operations.

BGP EVPN represents a modern approach to overlay control plane design, replacing legacy learning mechanisms with a robust, scalable, and intelligent protocol suite. By combining the power of BGP with Ethernet VPN extensions, it enables seamless connectivity, mobility, and policy enforcement across virtualized environments. Its widespread adoption and rich feature set make it a cornerstone of contemporary network architectures, supporting the transition to agile, programmable, and resilient infrastructure. Through its dynamic route distribution, redundancy features, and integration with encapsulation technologies, BGP EVPN empowers organizations to build overlay networks that meet the demands of modern applications, services, and operational models.

Multihoming and Redundancy in Overlay Networks

Multihoming and redundancy are essential components of modern overlay network designs, ensuring continuous availability, fault tolerance, and high performance in increasingly complex and distributed infrastructures. As organizations adopt virtualization, cloud computing, and distributed applications, networks must be designed to accommodate failures, support diverse paths for traffic, and ensure seamless service continuity. Overlay networks, by virtue of their abstraction and flexibility, are uniquely positioned to implement effective multihoming and redundancy strategies that span virtual and physical boundaries. These strategies allow endpoints to remain reachable even during component failures, improve load balancing, and contribute to a resilient and self-healing network fabric.

In traditional network architectures, redundancy is achieved by provisioning multiple physical paths and configuring routing protocols to detect and respond to failures. This approach, while effective, becomes increasingly complex when virtualized workloads and multi-tenant topologies are introduced. Overlay networks solve many of these challenges by decoupling logical connectivity from physical infrastructure, enabling the creation of resilient topologies without being limited by the constraints of the underlying hardware. Through tunneling protocols such as VXLAN, NVGRE, and GENEVE, overlay networks encapsulate tenant traffic into logical constructs that can traverse multiple physical paths without requiring changes to the applications or endpoints. This encapsulation provides the foundation for multihoming, where a single virtual endpoint can connect to multiple physical or logical network entry points simultaneously.

Multihoming in overlay networks ensures that a virtual machine, container, or virtual switch can maintain active connections to multiple edge devices or gateways. These connections can be used in either active-active or active-standby modes, depending on the application and policy requirements. In active-active scenarios, traffic is distributed across multiple links or paths, enabling load sharing and maximizing throughput. In active-standby scenarios, a primary path handles all traffic under normal conditions, while backup paths are activated only in the event of failure. Overlay networks can implement both modes dynamically, adapting to changes in network state and traffic patterns.

The benefits of multihoming extend beyond simple failover. By connecting to multiple fabric nodes or virtual switches, overlay endpoints can select the optimal path based on performance, policy, or availability. This capability supports traffic engineering and quality-of-service enforcement, allowing organizations to optimize the use of available bandwidth and minimize latency. When combined with software-defined networking controllers, overlay networks can monitor path performance in real time and adjust tunnel endpoints or routing decisions accordingly. This dynamic adaptation helps maintain consistent service levels, even under variable load or during partial infrastructure outages.

Redundancy in overlay networks is further enhanced through control plane mechanisms that maintain consistent forwarding information across the network. In designs that use BGP EVPN as the control plane, multihoming is natively supported through the use of Ethernet Segment Identifiers. An endpoint that connects to multiple leaf switches can advertise a common ESI, allowing the network to recognize these connections as belonging to the same logical entity. The control plane coordinates the distribution of traffic across these links and ensures that MAC address learning and forwarding remain stable during failover or link restoration. This approach prevents MAC flapping and avoids service disruption during transitions between active paths.

At the data plane level, redundancy is achieved through the use of encapsulation and tunneling mechanisms that allow traffic to be rerouted around failures. When a link or node becomes unavailable, overlay tunnels can be reestablished dynamically to alternative endpoints. Tunneling protocols do not rely on broadcast or spanning tree protocols, which can be slow to converge in traditional Layer 2 environments. Instead, they leverage underlay routing protocols such as OSPF or BGP to determine available paths, combined with encapsulation metadata that enables rapid redirection of traffic. This model provides fast convergence and minimal packet loss during failure events, supporting applications with stringent uptime requirements.

In environments that utilize distributed workloads, such as Kubernetes clusters or NFV deployments, redundancy must be implemented not only at the network level but also at the service and application layers. Overlay networks contribute to this model by enabling service endpoints to be reachable from multiple locations. For example, a service may be deployed on multiple pods across a cluster, with each pod connected to a different overlay tunnel. Load balancers and ingress controllers can direct traffic to any available instance, and if one instance fails, the overlay ensures that other paths remain active. This model of service-level redundancy builds on the network's multihoming capabilities to deliver resilient application experiences.

Operationally, multihoming and redundancy in overlay networks simplify infrastructure management by reducing the impact of maintenance and upgrades. Administrators can perform rolling updates on fabric switches, hypervisors, or edge gateways without affecting end-to-end connectivity. The overlay's ability to reroute traffic in real time ensures that services remain available even as physical components are temporarily taken offline. This capability is essential for maintaining uptime in mission-critical environments and supports continuous delivery and DevOps practices.

Overlay networks also support redundancy across geographic locations, enabling disaster recovery and cross-region availability. By establishing tunnels between data centers or cloud regions, organizations can replicate services and data while ensuring that clients can access them regardless of physical location. In the event of a regional failure, overlay tunnels automatically reroute traffic to available instances in other locations, maintaining business continuity. These tunnels can carry encrypted traffic and preserve tenant and policy context through encapsulated metadata, allowing security and compliance requirements to be met even during failover scenarios.

Monitoring and observability are crucial for managing multihoming and redundancy in overlay networks. Network administrators must have visibility into tunnel status, path performance, and endpoint availability to detect failures and verify that redundancy mechanisms are functioning as intended. Overlay-aware monitoring tools can track encapsulated flows, correlate them with underlay metrics, and alert on anomalies such as path degradation or tunnel flaps. This data is essential for capacity planning, root cause analysis, and optimizing the placement of services and workloads.

The combination of multihoming and redundancy transforms overlay networks into resilient, adaptive platforms that can sustain high availability and consistent performance under a wide range of conditions. These capabilities are not optional but necessary in modern infrastructures that support cloud-native applications, multi-tenant services, and globally distributed architectures. As networks continue to evolve to support faster, more dynamic workloads, the ability to provide seamless connectivity, even in the face of failures, will define the effectiveness and reliability of the network fabric. Overlay networks, empowered by advanced tunneling protocols and intelligent control planes, are at the forefront of this transformation, ensuring that connectivity is always available, even when the unexpected occurs.

Overlay Network Monitoring and Telemetry

Overlay network monitoring and telemetry have become essential elements in maintaining visibility, performance, and security within modern virtualized infrastructures. As data centers, service providers, and cloud platforms increasingly rely on overlay networks to abstract and virtualize the underlying physical infrastructure, traditional monitoring tools and methods no longer provide sufficient insight. Overlay networks add a layer of logical complexity that operates independently of physical topology, encapsulating traffic with additional headers, metadata, and identifiers that represent tenants, services, or application policies. This abstraction makes it more difficult to trace traffic paths, understand performance characteristics, and detect anomalies using legacy approaches that were designed for flat, physical Layer 2 or Layer 3 networks. To address this challenge, new monitoring and telemetry strategies have emerged that focus on both overlay-specific visibility and integration with the underlay network to deliver a comprehensive and coherent operational view.

In an overlay network, traffic is encapsulated using tunneling protocols such as VXLAN, NVGRE, or GENEVE. This encapsulation allows virtual machines, containers, or other endpoints to communicate across physical boundaries as if they were on the same logical network. However, the encapsulated packet hides the original headers, meaning that traditional tools placed in the physical network cannot easily inspect or analyze traffic flows at the tenant or application level. Furthermore, the metadata introduced by encapsulation protocols, especially in extensible formats like GENEVE, carries important contextual information that is not visible to legacy monitoring systems. Effective monitoring in this context requires visibility into both the outer transport headers and the inner payload, along with a deep understanding of how encapsulated flows traverse both overlay and underlay infrastructures.

One of the foundational requirements for overlay monitoring is the ability to collect telemetry data from tunnel endpoints, such as virtual switches, host NICs, or physical leaf switches. These devices are responsible for encapsulating and decapsulating overlay traffic and therefore have access to the full context of each flow. By instrumenting these endpoints to generate telemetry data, operators can capture metrics such as tunnel state, encapsulation errors, packet loss, jitter, and latency. In the case of protocols like GENEVE, additional metadata fields may carry telemetry information directly within the data plane. This allows in-band telemetry to accompany each packet, updating as it traverses the network and recording performance characteristics at each hop. The data collected can then be streamed to centralized telemetry systems for analysis, correlation, and visualization.

Overlay network telemetry is particularly useful for understanding east-west traffic within virtualized environments. Traditional perimeter-based monitoring focuses on north-south traffic entering or exiting the data center. However, in modern environments, the majority of traffic occurs between services and applications running within the infrastructure. This east-west traffic is often fully encapsulated and can traverse multiple hops without ever touching traditional inspection points. Overlay-aware monitoring tools can inspect encapsulated flows at the source and destination, providing insight into application communication patterns, service dependencies, and potential bottlenecks. These tools must decode encapsulation headers, interpret metadata, and associate flows with the appropriate virtual machines, containers, or tenant identifiers.

End-to-end visibility is another key objective of overlay network telemetry. Administrators need to trace traffic across the full path from source to destination, correlating overlay tunnels with underlay routes and physical interfaces. This requires integration between overlay telemetry and underlay monitoring systems. Tools that provide this integration can correlate flow records, interface counters, and routing data across both layers to detect inconsistencies, identify asymmetric routing, and pinpoint the root cause of performance issues. For example, a packet drop detected on an overlay tunnel may be caused by congestion on a specific underlay link. Without correlated telemetry, such issues can be difficult to diagnose and resolve. With correlated data, operators can see the full context of the problem and take targeted action.

Telemetry also plays a vital role in network security and anomaly detection within overlay networks. By collecting and analyzing flow data, systems can detect deviations from normal behavior, such as unexpected traffic between tenants, anomalous port usage, or sudden increases in packet loss. When combined with machine learning algorithms and threat intelligence feeds, telemetry can be used to identify potential attacks, compromised endpoints, or misconfigured policies. Because overlay networks support multi-tenancy and often host sensitive workloads, maintaining real-time visibility into security-relevant telemetry is critical for compliance, auditing, and incident response.

Scalability is an important consideration when designing telemetry systems for overlay networks. The volume of data generated by monitoring encapsulated traffic across hundreds or thousands of tunnels can be significant. Efficient data collection, aggregation, and sampling mechanisms must be used to ensure that telemetry systems do not overwhelm storage or processing resources. Technologies such as IPFIX, sFlow, and gNMI provide scalable mechanisms for exporting telemetry data from network devices. Streaming telemetry platforms can ingest this data in real time and perform analysis to provide dashboards, alerts, and automated responses. These platforms often include time-series databases, analytics engines, and visualization tools that support both historical and real-time monitoring use cases.

Automation is increasingly integrated with telemetry in overlay networks to support closed-loop operations. When telemetry systems detect a degradation in performance or a policy violation, automated workflows can be triggered to remediate the issue. This might involve rerouting traffic through alternative tunnels, scaling out additional application instances, or modifying firewall rules. Such automation reduces mean time to resolution and supports highly resilient and adaptive network behavior. For example, if latency on a particular tunnel exceeds a defined threshold, the SDN controller may dynamically select a different path or rebalance traffic to restore service levels. These feedback loops depend on timely and accurate telemetry data that reflects the current state of the network.

The evolution of overlay networking has fundamentally changed how networks are operated and monitored. Visibility is no longer optional but a foundational requirement for performance, security, and operational efficiency. Overlay network telemetry must be pervasive, real-time, and context-aware, providing insights that span virtual and physical boundaries. It must capture not only traditional metrics like throughput and error rates but also higher-level information about application behavior, service health, and policy compliance. As overlay networks continue to expand in scope and complexity, telemetry will remain at the heart of network operations, enabling proactive management, rapid troubleshooting, and intelligent automation in support of dynamic, virtualized infrastructures. Through effective monitoring and telemetry, overlay networks become not only more manageable but also more reliable, secure, and aligned with the needs of modern digital applications.

Challenges in Overlay Troubleshooting

Troubleshooting overlay networks presents a unique and often complex set of challenges for network operators and engineers. While overlays deliver significant benefits in terms of flexibility, scalability, and multi-tenancy, they also introduce layers of abstraction that obscure visibility and complicate root cause analysis. Unlike traditional flat networks where data paths are directly observable and the forwarding behavior is easier to map, overlay networks rely on tunneling protocols and encapsulation mechanisms that mask the underlying infrastructure and create new dependencies between virtual and physical components. As a result, identifying and resolving network issues in overlay environments requires a deep understanding of both the overlay and underlay layers, as well as the tools and processes needed to bridge the gap between them.

One of the primary challenges in overlay troubleshooting is the loss of visibility into individual packet paths. In traditional networks, tools such as traceroute, ping, and ARP inspection provide straightforward ways to track the journey of a packet and identify where it may be dropped or delayed. In an overlay network, traffic is encapsulated before it traverses the physical infrastructure. This encapsulation hides the original source and destination addresses from intermediate devices in the underlay, rendering traditional tools ineffective or misleading. For example, a traceroute run from within a virtual machine may show only the first hop before encapsulation, after which the packet appears to travel directly to a remote endpoint with no indication of the physical path it actually took.

Another significant difficulty arises from the distributed nature of overlay networks. Virtual machines, containers, and services can reside on any host within the fabric, and their locations may change frequently due to orchestration events, auto-scaling, or failover mechanisms. Overlay endpoints are typically implemented in software-based virtual switches that operate on hypervisors or container hosts, and these endpoints are responsible for encapsulating and decapsulating traffic. If a packet is dropped or delayed, it can be challenging to determine whether the issue lies in the virtual switch, the tunnel itself, or somewhere in the physical transport network. The lack of centralized forwarding state further complicates the process, as there is no single device that maintains a complete view of the network's behavior.

Misconfigurations are a common source of overlay network problems, and they can be difficult to detect without specialized tools. Overlay networks depend on correct tunnel endpoint mappings, consistent virtual network identifiers, and accurate routing and forwarding tables. A mismatch in any of these parameters can result in black holes, where traffic is silently discarded, or in loops and misrouted packets. These issues may not generate obvious alerts and can remain hidden until they impact application performance or availability. Furthermore, because overlay networks often coexist with underlay routing and switching protocols, errors in one layer can propagate or mask problems in the other, making it difficult to isolate the root cause without multi-layer correlation.

The dynamic nature of overlays also introduces timing-related issues. Because endpoints can move and tunnels can be recreated on demand, transient states may occur where control plane information has not yet converged or been synchronized across devices. During these periods, traffic may be misrouted, dropped, or subjected to unexpected delays. Troubleshooting such transient issues is particularly difficult because by the time logs are examined or diagnostic tests are run, the condition may have resolved, leaving no clear evidence of what occurred. Capturing ephemeral events requires real-time telemetry and logging at both the control and data plane levels, which is often lacking in default configurations.

Overlay protocols themselves can introduce troubleshooting complexity. VXLAN, NVGRE, and GENEVE each have different encapsulation formats and behaviors, and the choice of control plane—whether static configuration, flood-and-learn, or BGP EVPN—determines how endpoint information is propagated. In multi-vendor environments, interoperability issues may arise where devices interpret or implement overlay specifications differently. Inconsistent parsing of metadata, incorrect support for specific route types, or divergent control plane behaviors can result in subtle but impactful errors that are difficult to diagnose. Engineers must be intimately familiar with the specifications and operational nuances of each protocol in use, and they must be able to interpret packet captures at both the inner and outer layers of the encapsulated traffic.

Tools and processes for overlay troubleshooting are still maturing. Many legacy monitoring systems do not understand overlay headers or fail to correlate overlay and underlay metrics. While some modern telemetry platforms can ingest flow records, tunnel statistics, and endpoint events, there is often a lack of integration that makes it hard to construct an end-to-end view of a problem. Operators may need to manually piece together logs, configuration data, and packet traces from multiple sources to build a coherent picture. This process is time-consuming, prone to error, and requires a high level of expertise. Without sufficient automation and integration, the mean time to repair in overlay environments can be significantly longer than in traditional networks.

Another challenge is in maintaining security visibility during troubleshooting efforts. Because overlay networks often carry sensitive tenant traffic or segment services with strict policies, visibility tools must be carefully integrated to ensure they do not violate isolation boundaries or expose confidential data. Capturing traffic at tunnel endpoints must be done with authorization and awareness of tenant impact. Furthermore, the encapsulation of traffic can interfere with the operation of security appliances that rely on cleartext headers or payloads. Troubleshooting encrypted overlay traffic, especially when combined with end-to-end application encryption, adds an additional layer of difficulty, as traditional deep packet inspection is no longer effective.

Collaboration between network and application teams is also essential in overlay environments, as many network issues manifest as application-level problems and vice versa. Overlay networks blur the lines between infrastructure and application domains, making it important for network teams to understand application topologies, service dependencies, and orchestration behavior. At the same time, application developers must be aware of network policies, segmentation rules, and performance constraints imposed by the overlay. Troubleshooting often requires coordinated efforts across teams to interpret symptoms and trace them back to underlying causes that may reside in either domain.

Despite these challenges, advancements in observability, automation, and telemetry are gradually improving the ability to troubleshoot overlay networks. Integration between SDN controllers, orchestration platforms, and monitoring systems allows for more contextual and real-time diagnosis. Protocols such as gNMI and streaming telemetry provide continuous updates on tunnel health and endpoint status. Overlay-aware packet analyzers and flow visualizers can reconstruct encapsulated traffic paths and detect anomalies. With continued innovation in these areas, overlay troubleshooting will become more manageable, but the complexity inherent in virtualized, abstracted, and multi-layered networks will always require skilled analysis and comprehensive toolsets to ensure reliable operations.

Overlay Network Lab Design and Testing

Designing and testing an overlay network in a controlled lab environment is a critical step in validating architecture choices, exploring protocol behavior, and preparing for production deployment. Overlay networks introduce complex interactions between logical and physical layers, control planes and data planes, encapsulation protocols and routing domains. A well-structured lab allows engineers to simulate real-world topologies, experiment with different configurations, identify potential operational issues, and gain deep familiarity with how overlay components function together. The lab becomes a safe space for learning, troubleshooting, and stress-testing solutions before they impact live users or critical services.

To design an effective overlay network lab, it is important to begin by defining the scope and objectives of the testing environment. The lab should reflect the production architecture as closely as possible, including the overlay protocols to be used, the control plane architecture, the encapsulation formats, and the types of endpoints or workloads involved. Common protocols for overlay networking include VXLAN, GENEVE, and NVGRE, each with specific header structures, operational behaviors, and support requirements. Choosing the right protocol to model depends on the use case being tested, such as data center virtualization, multi-tenant cloud environments, or service chaining with virtual network functions.

A basic overlay network lab should include multiple virtual or physical hosts acting as tunnel endpoints. These endpoints can be implemented using virtual switches such as Open vSwitch or commercial hypervisor-based switches, as well as Linux-based network namespaces or container platforms like Kubernetes. These endpoints simulate the encapsulation and decapsulation of tenant traffic, allowing engineers to observe how the overlay fabric forms and behaves under different scenarios. The lab should also include simulated workloads such as virtual machines or containers that generate traffic, allowing for the testing of east-west communication across tunnels and the validation of network segmentation policies.

The underlay network, although not the focus of the overlay, must also be emulated to provide the necessary IP connectivity between tunnel endpoints. In the lab, this underlay can be implemented using simple IP routing between hosts, either with static routes or dynamic protocols like OSPF or BGP. It is essential that the underlay supports proper MTU sizes to accommodate encapsulated packets without fragmentation. Misconfigured MTU settings can lead to elusive packet drops and must be carefully tested. The ability to manipulate underlay conditions in the lab, such as simulating link failures, latency, or congestion, provides valuable insights into how overlay networks respond to real-world challenges.

A critical component of overlay network testing is the control plane. If using a flood-and-learn model, engineers must validate that MAC address learning and aging function as expected across tunnels. In more sophisticated setups using BGP EVPN as a control plane, routers and switches running BGP must be configured to advertise the appropriate EVPN route types, including MAC/IP bindings and IP prefix routes. This allows the overlay fabric to dynamically build forwarding tables without relying on broadcast traffic. The lab should include route reflectors, redundant peers, and failover scenarios to test how the control plane reacts to topology changes and how quickly it converges.

Another area of focus in the overlay lab is the policy and security model. Overlay networks enable fine-grained control of traffic between endpoints, typically using ACLs, security groups, or network policies enforced at the virtual switch level. Testing these policies in the lab ensures that segmentation rules are correctly applied and enforced. Scenarios to test include legitimate communication between workloads in the same virtual network, blocked traffic between different tenants, and exceptions such as shared services or gateways. Additionally, labs can validate microsegmentation configurations, where each workload may have its own set of ingress and egress rules based on labels or identity.

Performance testing is also a key objective in overlay labs. Encapsulation introduces additional processing overhead and increased packet size, which can impact throughput, latency, and CPU utilization. By generating synthetic traffic with tools such as iperf, hping, or custom scripts, engineers can measure how the overlay performs under different load conditions. These tests should include both small and large packet sizes, varying connection counts, and bi-directional flows. In labs that support hardware offload, comparing software and hardware performance provides insight into the benefits of SmartNICs or DPDK acceleration in production deployments.

Observability and telemetry are indispensable in the lab. Engineers should implement monitoring tools that capture flow records, tunnel statistics, and performance metrics. These tools might include open-source platforms such as Prometheus, Grafana, ELK Stack, or commercial network visibility solutions. Packet capture utilities like tcpdump or Wireshark are particularly valuable in overlay environments, as they allow inspection of both the outer and inner headers, revealing how traffic is encapsulated, routed, and decapsulated. For advanced protocols like GENEVE, capturing and decoding the option fields reveals how metadata is propagated through the network and how it might be used for service chaining or policy enforcement.

Troubleshooting is an ongoing part of lab testing. Common issues that arise include MTU mismatches, incorrect tunnel endpoint configurations, BGP session failures, policy misconfigurations, and control plane convergence delays. By documenting these problems and their resolutions, engineers create a knowledge base that will be invaluable when the overlay is deployed in production. Simulating failure conditions such as link flaps, node crashes, or misadvertised routes tests the resilience of the overlay and the ability of the network to self-heal.

Finally, overlay labs should evolve with the needs of the network. As new features are introduced, such as service function chaining, integration with Kubernetes, or support for encryption and telemetry, the lab provides a platform to test these capabilities in isolation before rolling them out widely. Labs also support continuous learning and training, allowing new team members to gain hands-on experience with overlay technologies in a risk-free environment. In high-performing network teams, the lab is treated as a living system—updated regularly, integrated into automation pipelines, and used to validate changes before they reach production.

Building a comprehensive overlay network lab provides a foundation for successful deployment and operation. It offers a realistic environment where engineers can simulate real-world challenges, test resilience and performance, and develop confidence in their configurations and architectures. As networks become more abstracted, programmable, and distributed, the lab becomes the primary interface between design and reality, ensuring that overlay networks deliver on their promise of agility, scalability, and operational excellence.

Automation and Orchestration of Overlay Networks

Automation and orchestration have become indispensable in the management of overlay networks as organizations strive to operate agile, scalable, and highly available infrastructure. The complexity of overlay networking, driven by virtualization, cloud computing, and microservices architecture, demands a level of operational efficiency that cannot be achieved through manual configuration and reactive troubleshooting. Overlay networks introduce multiple layers of abstraction between workloads and the physical network, and they often span across heterogeneous environments composed of various platforms, hypervisors, container orchestrators, and physical infrastructure. This abstraction provides great flexibility, but it also requires advanced tools and workflows to manage network provisioning, policy enforcement, and lifecycle management at scale.

Overlay networks operate by creating logical paths between endpoints, encapsulating traffic in protocols like VXLAN, NVGRE, or GENEVE to allow workloads in different physical locations or IP subnets to communicate as though they were on the same Layer 2 network. While this simplifies network design from an application perspective, managing these logical networks manually becomes unsustainable as the number of endpoints, tenants, and policies grows. Each new virtual machine, container, or service may require the creation or modification of tunnels, routing entries, access control policies, and monitoring configurations. Without automation, this operational burden leads to errors, configuration drift, and increased time to deployment.

Automation addresses these challenges by enabling repeatable and consistent configuration of overlay network components using scripts, templates, and infrastructure-as-code practices. With automation tools such as Ansible, Terraform, and Python-based frameworks, administrators can define overlay topologies declaratively and push changes across the environment with minimal human intervention. These tools allow network configurations to be version-controlled, audited, and integrated into continuous integration and continuous deployment pipelines. Overlay tunnel provisioning, VNI allocation, endpoint registration, and policy application can all be automated to occur alongside the deployment of workloads, ensuring that the network adapts as applications scale up or down.

Orchestration extends the power of automation by managing the dependencies and coordination between different components of the infrastructure. Orchestrators such as Kubernetes, OpenStack, and VMware vRealize Automation provide control over compute, storage, and networking resources, ensuring that virtual networks are provisioned in sync with virtual machines, containers, and other application components. When a new workload is created through an orchestrator, it can automatically trigger the creation of the necessary overlay network elements, including virtual interfaces, security groups, and routes. This tight integration enables policy-driven automation, where decisions about network topology and access control are derived from high-level service definitions and application metadata.

Controllers play a central role in the automation and orchestration of overlay networks. In software-defined networking architectures, the controller maintains a centralized view of the network state and is responsible for programming forwarding decisions into the data plane. Controllers such as OpenDaylight, OVN, or vendor-specific platforms manage overlay networks by maintaining tunnel mappings, distributing MAC and IP address information, and enforcing segmentation policies. Through APIs, these controllers expose interfaces to orchestration platforms and automation tools, allowing the entire overlay fabric to be managed programmatically. Controllers also abstract the complexity of underlying protocols, enabling automation systems to work at a higher level of abstraction without needing to manage individual encapsulation details or flow tables.

Policy automation is another crucial aspect of overlay orchestration. Modern overlay networks support granular policy definitions that govern traffic between workloads based on identity, tags, or application roles. These policies can be defined once and applied dynamically to workloads as they are created. For example, a policy might specify that database containers can only communicate with backend services on specific ports. When a new container is launched and tagged accordingly, the orchestrator and network controller apply the correct policy without requiring manual input. This model supports microsegmentation and zero-trust networking, where access is restricted by default and only explicitly permitted traffic is allowed.

Monitoring and telemetry are also integrated into automated overlay environments. Tools that collect metrics, logs, and traces can be configured as part of the deployment process to ensure that every workload is instrumented from the moment it is provisioned. Automation scripts can configure telemetry agents, establish log forwarding pipelines, and tag data based on the overlay context such as tenant ID or service name. This automation ensures that observability is not an afterthought but a built-in feature of the network infrastructure. Anomalies or performance degradations can be detected early, and corrective actions can be initiated automatically through event-driven automation or closed-loop systems.

Security automation is vital in overlay networks where the perimeter is no longer a single point of enforcement. With workloads distributed across multiple hosts, clouds, and regions, security policies must follow the workloads and adapt to changing contexts. Automated overlay networks support the dynamic insertion of security services such as firewalls, intrusion detection systems, and service proxies based on traffic classification or threat detection. Orchestration tools can determine the need for security inspection based on the type of service or sensitivity of the data and configure the overlay to redirect traffic through the appropriate functions. This enables a flexible and adaptive security model that aligns with the agility of cloud-native applications.

In multi-tenant environments, automation ensures consistent enforcement of isolation boundaries and resource limits. Each tenant may require its own set of overlay networks, address spaces, and security policies. Automation tools can dynamically allocate VNIs, configure tenant-specific routing, and apply role-based access controls to ensure that tenants remain isolated and that their resources are governed by quotas and policies. Tenants can also be given self-service portals or APIs to manage their own virtual networks within the constraints defined by the provider, enabling autonomy without compromising operational control.

As overlay networks continue to evolve and expand into hybrid and multi-cloud environments, the importance of automation and orchestration grows. Cross-domain orchestration allows workloads to be moved between on-premises data centers and public cloud platforms while preserving network policies and identities. Overlay tunnels can be automatically established between clouds, and policies can be federated to ensure consistent access control and segmentation. Tools like HashiCorp Consul, Cisco ACI, or VMware NSX support cross-environment integration and provide the abstractions necessary to manage overlays that span diverse infrastructures.

The journey to full automation of overlay networks involves not only adopting the right tools but also rethinking operational models. Teams must embrace declarative configuration, CI/CD practices, and collaborative workflows between network, security, and application domains. Training and documentation become essential to ensure that automation scripts and orchestration logic are understood, maintained, and improved over time. Governance frameworks should be implemented to ensure that automation does not inadvertently violate compliance or operational standards.

Automation and orchestration transform overlay networking from a manually intensive, error-prone process into a predictable, scalable, and resilient system. They enable networks to keep pace with the rapid change of digital applications, support complex policies and services, and deliver the performance and reliability that users expect. As the foundation of modern infrastructure, overlay networks must be as dynamic as the applications they support, and only through automation can that level of adaptability be achieved.

Overlay Networks and Network Slicing

Overlay networks have emerged as a foundational technology in the evolution of network slicing, particularly in the context of 5G, edge computing, and multi-tenant cloud infrastructures. Network slicing refers to the ability to partition a physical network into multiple isolated virtual networks, or slices, each tailored to the specific requirements of different services, applications, or users. These slices operate as independent networks with dedicated resources and policies, allowing service providers and enterprises to deliver highly customized connectivity experiences over shared infrastructure. Overlay networks enable the implementation of network slicing by abstracting the physical topology and creating logical topologies that can be dynamically instantiated, managed, and secured without requiring modifications to the underlying transport fabric.

The concept of network slicing is deeply aligned with the principles of virtualization and programmability. Each network slice must provide guaranteed performance, security, and isolation, while being agile enough to adapt to dynamic workload and service demands. Overlay networks fulfill these requirements by encapsulating tenant or service traffic within tunnels that carry identifiers, metadata, and policies which define the characteristics of each slice. Encapsulation protocols like VXLAN and GENEVE allow for this traffic to be segmented and steered across a shared physical network without losing slice-specific context. The encapsulated headers serve as a logical demarcation between slices, ensuring that traffic belonging to one slice is never visible or accessible to another.

In the context of 5G, network slicing becomes especially critical. The 5G architecture is designed to support a wide range of services with vastly different requirements, from enhanced mobile broadband and massive machine-type communications to ultra-reliable low-latency applications. Each of these service types has unique performance, reliability, and security needs. A single physical 5G infrastructure must be capable of hosting all of them simultaneously without compromising service quality. Overlay networks play a key role in achieving this by creating isolated transport slices that align with the core, transport, and access components of the 5G network. These slices span multiple domains, including the data center, edge, and radio access network, and must be coordinated end to end to deliver a seamless service experience.

Overlay-based network slices can be designed with specific parameters for bandwidth, latency, jitter, and resiliency. For example, a slice supporting autonomous vehicles may require ultra-low latency and high reliability, while another slice supporting video streaming may prioritize high throughput. These parameters can be encoded into the overlay metadata, enabling intermediate devices to make forwarding decisions based on the slice context. With advanced overlay protocols like GENEVE, it becomes possible to include service-level information directly within the encapsulation headers, allowing for policy enforcement, traffic steering, and monitoring that is tightly coupled to the slice definition.

The isolation provided by overlay networks ensures that faults, congestion, or security breaches in one slice do not affect others. This is achieved through dedicated forwarding tables, unique tunnel identifiers, and strict enforcement of access control policies at tunnel endpoints. In multi-tenant environments, where different organizations share the same infrastructure, this isolation becomes a fundamental requirement. Overlay networks can enforce tenant-level boundaries that prevent data leakage or unauthorized access, while also enabling administrators to allocate resources per slice based on contractual agreements or service-level objectives.

Orchestration is a crucial enabler of network slicing in overlay environments. Slice creation, scaling, and teardown must be automated and driven by high-level intent, rather than manual configuration. Orchestration platforms interact with SDN controllers and network function managers to provision the necessary tunnels, endpoints, and policies that define a slice. This includes allocating identifiers such as VNIs, configuring control plane elements like BGP EVPN for dynamic learning, and integrating security functions such as firewalls or intrusion prevention systems within the slice. Automation ensures that slices can be provisioned on demand, adapt to changes in traffic patterns, and be decommissioned when no longer needed, thereby optimizing the use of infrastructure resources.

Another dimension of network slicing enabled by overlay networks is multi-domain and multi-access integration. Slices often need to span across data centers, core networks, edge locations, and access networks such as Wi-Fi, LTE, or 5G. Overlay tunnels can bridge these diverse environments, creating a unified logical network that maintains consistent policy and visibility. This is essential in use cases such as industrial IoT, where devices may connect over different types of access networks but require a common operational and security framework. By encapsulating traffic at the edge and maintaining slice context throughout the transport network, overlay networks ensure seamless connectivity and control across all domains.

Observability is another critical factor in managing network slices over overlays. Administrators must be able to monitor the performance and health of each slice independently, detecting anomalies and enforcing compliance with service-level agreements. Overlay telemetry, especially when integrated with extensible protocols like GENEVE, allows for in-band collection of metrics such as latency, packet loss, and path utilization. These metrics can be tagged with slice identifiers and exported to centralized analytics platforms, providing real-time and historical views of slice performance. This observability supports closed-loop automation, where slice behavior is continuously optimized based on telemetry data and business policy.

Security considerations are paramount in overlay-based network slicing. Since multiple slices coexist on the same infrastructure, each slice must be protected against unauthorized access, data exfiltration, and interference from others. Overlay networks support per-slice encryption, authentication of tunnel endpoints, and dynamic security policy enforcement. Network functions such as firewalls, encryption gateways, and deep packet inspection engines can be instantiated per slice, either as virtual functions or integrated into smart NICs and service meshes. These functions can operate on slice-specific metadata to enforce tailored security policies that align with the service's sensitivity and regulatory requirements.

Overlay networks also support the elasticity and mobility required by modern applications. Slices must be able to follow workloads as they move between regions, scale with user demand, and recover from failures without service interruption. By abstracting the physical transport and leveraging tunneling for logical connectivity, overlays ensure that slice endpoints remain reachable regardless of where they are instantiated. This is particularly important for edge applications and mobile services, where user proximity and latency optimization drive frequent workload relocation.

The convergence of overlay networking and network slicing represents a shift toward intent-driven, service-centric network architecture. Rather than provisioning static paths and infrastructure, operators define service requirements and rely on overlays to instantiate the necessary connectivity and policies dynamically. This transformation empowers service providers to deliver differentiated services with precision, agility, and efficiency. As applications become more diverse and latency-sensitive, and as infrastructure becomes more distributed, the ability to deliver dedicated, optimized network experiences over shared physical assets becomes a competitive necessity. Overlay networks provide the technological foundation to realize this vision, bringing network slicing from a theoretical concept into practical, scalable deployment.

Hybrid Cloud Overlay Networking

Hybrid cloud overlay networking has become a cornerstone of modern enterprise architecture, enabling seamless connectivity, security, and scalability across private data centers and public cloud environments. As organizations adopt hybrid cloud strategies to combine the control and compliance of on-premises infrastructure with the agility and elasticity of cloud services, the network must evolve to support consistent connectivity between diverse environments. Overlay networking provides the abstraction layer necessary to unify these disparate domains, allowing applications and services to communicate as though they were part of a single, integrated infrastructure. By encapsulating traffic and isolating it through virtual network identifiers and metadata, overlay networks bridge the gaps between clouds, enabling secure and dynamic workload mobility.

At the heart of hybrid cloud overlay networking is the principle of decoupling logical connectivity from physical infrastructure. Traditional networking relies on physical routers, switches, and firewalls to route and control traffic based on IP subnets and VLANs. In a hybrid cloud, where workloads are distributed across multiple physical and virtual environments, this approach quickly becomes inadequate. Overlay networks overcome these limitations by creating virtual tunnels between endpoints, encapsulating traffic in protocols like VXLAN or GENEVE. These tunnels form the backbone of a virtualized network that spans across cloud and on-premises resources, providing end-to-end communication without the need to reconfigure the underlay network.

One of the primary benefits of hybrid cloud overlay networking is the ability to maintain consistent network policies and segmentation across environments. In a traditional model, extending VLANs from on-premises data centers to the cloud is either impractical or unsupported, forcing administrators to rearchitect their applications or expose sensitive traffic to the public internet. Overlay networks, by contrast, allow administrators to define segmentation policies using virtual network identifiers and enforce them uniformly regardless of location. A workload in a private data center can communicate securely with a peer in the public cloud over an encrypted overlay tunnel, with both endpoints participating in the same virtual network. This consistency simplifies security management, reduces configuration errors, and accelerates deployment timelines.

Security is a critical concern in hybrid cloud environments, and overlay networking plays a significant role in maintaining a secure posture. Because overlay networks operate independently of the underlying infrastructure, they can be encrypted end-to-end using IPsec, TLS, or other secure tunneling protocols. Traffic is encapsulated at the source and decapsulated only at the destination, making it invisible to intermediate devices and reducing the risk of interception. Overlay tunnels can be authenticated using certificates or key-based mechanisms to ensure that only authorized endpoints participate in the virtual network. Additionally, security policies such as microsegmentation can be enforced based on overlay metadata, allowing granular control over traffic flows between services.

Hybrid cloud overlay networking also enables workload mobility, a key benefit of hybrid architectures. Organizations often need to migrate workloads between on-premises and cloud environments for cost optimization, disaster recovery, or performance optimization. Without overlays, such migrations require complex reconfiguration of routing, security policies, and DNS. With overlays in place, workloads retain their IP addresses and security policies even as they move, because the overlay abstracts the underlying location. The network simply reestablishes the necessary tunnels and updates endpoint mappings through the control plane. This enables seamless live migrations and hybrid deployments where components of a single application reside in different clouds.

Another advantage of overlay networks in hybrid cloud is the ability to implement unified control and orchestration. Modern overlay solutions are tightly integrated with orchestration platforms like Kubernetes, OpenStack, and cloud-native APIs. This integration allows administrators to define infrastructure as code, using declarative models to provision networks, enforce policies, and monitor traffic. When a new application is deployed, the orchestration platform can automatically configure the necessary overlay tunnels, apply segmentation policies, and register endpoints with the control plane. This level of automation reduces operational overhead and ensures that hybrid cloud networks remain aligned with business objectives and security requirements.

Performance and reliability are important considerations in hybrid cloud overlay networking. Because traffic between environments often traverses the public internet or shared wide area networks, it is subject to variable latency and packet loss. Overlay networks can mitigate these issues by supporting dynamic path selection, load balancing, and congestion avoidance. Some implementations use intelligent routing algorithms or integrate with software-defined WAN solutions to optimize traffic flows based on real-time network conditions. Additionally, encapsulation headers can include telemetry data that provides visibility into tunnel performance, allowing administrators to identify and resolve issues proactively.

Hybrid cloud overlays also facilitate the integration of legacy and modern systems. Many enterprises have applications that span generations of infrastructure, from mainframes and virtual machines to containers and serverless functions. Overlay networks provide a common connectivity framework that bridges these differences, enabling older systems to communicate with cloud-native services without the need for complex network translation or proxying. This integration supports digital transformation initiatives by allowing organizations to modernize their infrastructure incrementally while maintaining service continuity.

As hybrid cloud environments grow in complexity, observability becomes essential. Overlay networks support advanced telemetry and monitoring capabilities that provide deep visibility into traffic flows, tunnel health, and application performance. By embedding metadata into encapsulated packets, overlay protocols allow administrators to trace traffic across domains, correlate events, and enforce compliance. Integration with logging, metrics, and alerting systems enables real-time monitoring and root cause analysis. This observability is crucial for maintaining service levels, detecting anomalies, and ensuring the overall health of the hybrid network.

Compliance and governance are additional areas where hybrid cloud overlay networking provides value. Regulatory requirements often mandate strict controls over where data resides and how it is transmitted. Overlay networks enable organizations to enforce geographic and policy boundaries by controlling how traffic flows between environments. For example, a financial application may require that customer data remain within a specific region. Using overlay tunnels and segmentation, administrators can ensure that traffic never leaves the approved geography, satisfying compliance mandates while maintaining operational flexibility.

Overlay networks are not a one-size-fits-all solution, and designing an effective hybrid cloud overlay architecture requires careful consideration of use cases, performance requirements, and integration points. Different applications may require different overlay configurations, with some prioritizing low latency, others requiring high security, and still others focusing on ease of deployment. A successful hybrid cloud overlay strategy involves collaboration between networking, security, application, and operations teams to define policies, select technologies, and implement automation that aligns with the organization's goals.

Hybrid cloud overlay networking is the connective tissue of modern IT infrastructure, enabling organizations to span environments, enforce consistent policies, and deliver agile, secure, and high-performance services across domains. It abstracts complexity, enhances flexibility, and supports a unified operational model that empowers businesses to innovate without being constrained by traditional network boundaries. As enterprises continue to expand their presence across private and public clouds, overlay networking will remain a critical enabler of hybrid strategies, providing the foundation for scalable, resilient, and intelligent connectivity in an increasingly distributed world.

Overlay Networking Best Practices

Implementing overlay networking in a modern data center or cloud environment requires more than just selecting the right protocol or deploying virtual tunnels. To ensure that overlay networks operate efficiently, securely, and at scale, network architects and operators must follow a set of best practices that guide everything from design and deployment to monitoring and troubleshooting. Overlay networking introduces a powerful abstraction layer that enables flexibility, multi-tenancy, and workload mobility, but this same abstraction also increases the complexity of managing connectivity, visibility, and control. Following established best practices helps reduce this complexity, avoid common pitfalls, and deliver a stable and resilient network infrastructure that meets the needs of both developers and operations teams.

A foundational best practice in overlay networking is to design with the underlay in mind. Overlay networks depend entirely on the physical transport provided by the underlay, and any weaknesses in the underlay will be amplified by the overlay. A well-architected underlay should use a scalable and deterministic design, such as a leaf-spine topology, with consistent MTU settings and support for equal-cost multipath routing. MTU mismatches are a frequent source of packet drops in overlay networks because the encapsulated packets are larger than the original payload. Ensuring that every hop in the underlay supports jumbo frames that can handle encapsulated traffic without fragmentation is essential for maintaining performance and avoiding silent failures.

Overlay networks should also be built with a clear and consistent segmentation strategy. Logical isolation between tenants, environments, or applications should be enforced using mechanisms such as VNIs, tenant identifiers, or other metadata provided by the overlay protocol. Each segment must be uniquely identifiable, and policies should be put in place to control traffic between segments. In multi-tenant or service-oriented environments, this segmentation forms the foundation of security, compliance, and operational integrity. Administrators should maintain an inventory of all overlay segments, ensure they are mapped appropriately to applications or services, and regularly audit configurations to prevent unauthorized cross-segment communication.

When selecting an overlay protocol, it is important to consider interoperability, feature support, and extensibility. VXLAN is widely adopted and supported by a broad range of hardware and software platforms, making it a strong choice for environments that require compatibility and simplicity. GENEVE, while newer, offers greater flexibility by supporting optional metadata fields that can be used for service chaining, telemetry, and policy enforcement. Regardless of the protocol, it is best to avoid mixing encapsulation formats unless there is a well-defined interworking strategy. Using a single overlay protocol across the environment simplifies troubleshooting, reduces configuration errors, and enhances the effectiveness of monitoring tools.

Control plane design is another critical consideration. Overlays that rely on flood-and-learn behavior can scale poorly and create unnecessary broadcast traffic, which increases the load on both the overlay and underlay. Instead, it is recommended to deploy a control plane such as BGP EVPN to distribute endpoint reachability information dynamically and efficiently. A distributed control plane minimizes convergence times during failover, improves stability, and supports advanced features like multi-homing and MAC mobility. It is essential to test control plane behavior under failure conditions, such as link loss or node restarts, to ensure that the network can recover quickly and without manual intervention.

Operational visibility is often one of the most challenging aspects of managing overlay networks, so it is vital to implement observability from the start. Traditional monitoring tools may not provide visibility into encapsulated traffic, so overlay-specific telemetry should be integrated into the architecture. Tools that can decode VXLAN or GENEVE headers, correlate flow records across overlay and underlay layers, and provide real-time insights into tunnel health are invaluable.

Packet capture capabilities at tunnel endpoints, combined with analytics platforms that can visualize flows and anomalies, enable faster troubleshooting and performance tuning. In environments that support it, in-band telemetry allows performance data to travel alongside user traffic, providing an accurate picture of latency, jitter, and loss in real time.

Automation is a best practice that cannot be overlooked. As overlay networks grow in scale and complexity, manual configuration becomes a liability. Infrastructure as code should be used to define overlay segments, tunnel endpoints, policies, and telemetry configurations. Automation tools such as Ansible, Terraform, or platform-specific orchestrators allow these configurations to be deployed reliably, tracked in version control, and applied consistently across environments. Automated testing and validation should be integrated into change management processes to ensure that new configurations do not introduce errors or regressions.

Security should be embedded into the design of the overlay from the outset. Microsegmentation enables fine-grained control of traffic between workloads, and these policies should be based on logical attributes such as tags, roles, or identities rather than static IP addresses. Overlay metadata can be used to enforce context-aware policies that adapt as workloads move or scale. Encryption of overlay traffic is another essential practice, particularly in hybrid or multi-cloud environments where data traverses untrusted networks. End-to-end encryption between tunnel endpoints ensures that traffic cannot be intercepted or modified in transit, protecting both data integrity and privacy.

Change control and documentation are vital for long-term success. Overlay networks can become opaque if their logical topologies, segmentation policies, and tunnel configurations are not clearly documented and maintained. Operators should maintain diagrams, inventories, and policy definitions that reflect the current state of the overlay. Changes should be reviewed through structured processes that include impact analysis, rollback planning, and validation testing. Logging and audit trails should be enabled to track configuration changes and support forensic investigations if necessary.

Training and knowledge sharing also contribute to the effectiveness of overlay network operations. Because overlays introduce new concepts and tools, teams must invest in continuous education to keep skills aligned with evolving technologies. Cross-functional collaboration between networking, security, and application teams ensures that overlays are configured and used effectively. Regular tabletop exercises, lab simulations, and post-mortem reviews help teams refine their processes and improve response times.

Overlay networks are a transformative technology that enable agility, scalability, and security in modern infrastructures. However, they also introduce complexity that must be managed through deliberate design and disciplined operations. By adhering to best practices across architecture, control plane configuration, monitoring, automation, and security, organizations can unlock the full potential of overlay networking while minimizing risk and maintaining operational excellence. These practices serve not only as technical guidelines but also as the foundation for building resilient and future-ready networks that support the demands of digital transformation.

Case Study: VXLAN in a Large Data Center

In the context of modern data centers, the need for scalable, flexible, and efficient networking solutions has become paramount. Traditional Layer 2 technologies such as VLANs have proven insufficient to support the growth and complexity of current multi-tenant environments, particularly in scenarios where virtualization and cloud-native applications dominate. One of the most transformative technologies to address these challenges is VXLAN, or Virtual Extensible LAN. This case study explores the deployment of VXLAN in a large-scale enterprise data center that required high levels of scalability, tenant isolation, and support for workload mobility across hundreds of physical and virtual hosts.

The organization in question operates a regional data center that supports more than 10,000 virtual machines across a hybrid infrastructure composed of hypervisors, bare-metal servers, and container platforms. The existing network architecture relied heavily on VLAN-based segmentation, with a traditional three-tier topology that included access, aggregation, and core layers. As the demand for isolated environments for different business units and projects grew, network administrators faced limitations in the 4096 VLAN ID cap, inflexible network provisioning processes, and a lack of support for dynamic workload placement. In response to these limitations, the organization began designing an overlay network strategy using VXLAN as the encapsulation protocol, combined with BGP EVPN as the control plane to manage endpoint reachability.

The new design adopted a spine-leaf topology to provide a high-bandwidth, low-latency fabric. Each leaf switch functioned as a VXLAN Tunnel Endpoint, or VTEP, capable of encapsulating and decapsulating traffic between virtual and physical workloads. The spine switches provided pure IP transport, unaware of the VXLAN encapsulated payloads. This design ensured high availability and path diversity, while VXLAN overlays allowed for the creation of logical Layer 2 segments that could span multiple racks or even data halls without the need for traditional VLAN trunking. The deployment supported both VLAN-to-VXLAN bridging for legacy workloads and fully routed VXLAN segments for cloud-native services.

One of the major implementation challenges was the configuration of VTEPs across the network. Each hypervisor and top-of-rack switch required a consistent configuration of VXLAN IDs, VNIs, and BGP sessions to the EVPN route reflectors. Automation played a key role in addressing this complexity. The organization used Ansible to automate the configuration of VXLAN parameters, ensuring that each new tenant or workload segment was assigned a unique VNI and that the associated route advertisements were propagated correctly. BGP EVPN route types 2 and 3 were used extensively to advertise MAC and IP address bindings, as well as multicast group associations for efficient broadcast, unknown unicast, and multicast traffic handling.

Security and segmentation were critical goals of the deployment. The VXLAN design allowed for complete tenant isolation through the use of separate VNIs and associated policies enforced at the virtual switch layer. Network policies were implemented using distributed firewalls within the hypervisor, with additional access control enforced by leaf switches based on source and destination VNIs. For east-west traffic between virtual machines, the policy model ensured that only explicitly allowed communications could take place. Microsegmentation was extended to container workloads through the integration of a container networking interface that supported VXLAN tunneling and policy enforcement using Kubernetes network policies.

To validate the performance and stability of the new overlay, the team conducted extensive testing in a staging environment. Synthetic workloads were generated to simulate production traffic patterns, including bursty traffic flows, high-concurrency connections, and service discovery operations. The team measured throughput, latency, and jitter across VXLAN tunnels, comparing results against baseline measurements taken from the legacy VLAN infrastructure. The results demonstrated improved path utilization, reduced convergence time during failover events, and significantly better support for large numbers of isolated tenants. Hardware offloading of VXLAN encapsulation was enabled on supported NICs and switches, further enhancing performance by reducing CPU overhead on hosts.

Monitoring and observability were also significantly enhanced in the VXLAN deployment. The organization deployed flow telemetry tools that could inspect VXLAN headers, providing visibility into tenant-specific traffic and tunnel health. These tools were integrated with existing logging and alerting systems, allowing operators to detect tunnel flaps, MAC mobility events, and route convergence delays in real time. Dashboards were created to visualize overlay traffic patterns, tunnel utilization, and VNI-specific metrics, enabling proactive troubleshooting and capacity planning. Packet captures taken at VTEP interfaces allowed for deep inspection of encapsulated and decapsulated frames, supporting efficient root cause analysis during service incidents.

One particularly successful aspect of the deployment was the support for workload mobility. With VXLAN and BGP EVPN, virtual machines could be migrated between hypervisors or racks without losing network connectivity or requiring reconfiguration. The control plane dynamically updated MAC/IP bindings as workloads moved, and the distributed nature of the VTEPs ensured that traffic was always routed to the correct destination without looping or black holing. This mobility supported the organization's goal of implementing live migration for maintenance and dynamic scaling, reducing downtime and improving resource utilization.

Scalability was another key benefit of VXLAN in this large data center. The 24-bit VNI field allowed the creation of over 16 million unique overlay segments, far exceeding the limitations of traditional VLANs. This scalability enabled the organization to onboard new tenants, projects, and environments without fear of exhausting segmentation identifiers. The BGP EVPN control plane handled route distribution efficiently, even as the number of advertised MAC and IP addresses grew into the tens of thousands. Route reflectors were scaled horizontally, and BGP peering sessions were managed dynamically through route server functionality to reduce configuration complexity.

Over the course of a year, the VXLAN overlay network proved to be robust, efficient, and flexible. It supported the organization's shift toward infrastructure as code, DevOps workflows, and hybrid cloud integration. Applications deployed across on-premises infrastructure and public cloud environments maintained seamless connectivity through VXLAN tunnels extended via IPsec gateways. The abstraction provided by VXLAN allowed developers to focus on application logic while the network team ensured security, performance, and compliance behind the scenes.

The deployment of VXLAN in this large data center represented a transformative shift in how network services were delivered. It enabled a high degree of agility without sacrificing control, simplified operations through automation and centralized policy, and laid the foundation for future integration with software-defined WAN, cloud-native networking, and intent-based automation. By embracing overlay networking at scale, the organization not only solved immediate challenges of segmentation and scalability but also positioned itself to adapt rapidly to the evolving demands of modern IT.

Case Study: NVGRE in a Microsoft Environment

Network Virtualization using Generic Routing Encapsulation, known as NVGRE, represents one of the earliest overlay networking technologies developed to address the limitations of traditional Layer 2 segmentation in virtualized environments. Designed by Microsoft to integrate closely with its suite of enterprise virtualization tools, NVGRE has been primarily deployed in environments based on Hyper-V, System Center, and Windows Server technologies. This case study explores the deployment of NVGRE in a large enterprise organization that had standardized on the Microsoft stack and was seeking to improve scalability, workload isolation, and network management flexibility across its private cloud infrastructure.

The enterprise operated several data centers, each hosting hundreds of Hyper-V servers running thousands of virtual machines for internal applications, development environments, and customer-facing services. Prior to adopting NVGRE, the organization relied on VLANs for tenant segmentation and traffic isolation, configured manually across physical switches and virtual switches within the Hyper-V hosts. As the number of business units and departments requiring isolated environments increased, the VLAN approach began to show its limitations. The finite number of VLAN IDs, combined with the operational overhead of configuring VLAN trunks on each switch, created a bottleneck that hindered the agility of provisioning new services and tenants.

Recognizing these challenges, the IT department decided to implement Microsoft's network virtualization solution using NVGRE as the overlay protocol. This decision aligned well with the existing investment in Microsoft technologies and allowed for tight integration with System Center Virtual Machine Manager, which would serve as the central orchestration tool for deploying and managing virtual networks. NVGRE provided a mechanism to encapsulate Layer 2 Ethernet frames within GRE tunnels that could traverse the IP-based underlay infrastructure. Each virtual network was assigned a unique Tenant Network Identifier, or TNI, a 24-bit field embedded in the GRE key field, ensuring logical isolation between tenant traffic over the shared physical infrastructure.

The implementation began with the deployment of the Network Virtualization Generic Routing Encapsulation (NVGRE) extensions on all Hyper-V hosts. These extensions enabled the virtual switch within Hyper-V to function as a virtualized network endpoint, capable of encapsulating and decapsulating NVGRE packets. Each host also ran a Network Virtualization Provider Address (PA) and Customer Address (CA) mapping service, allowing virtual machines to retain their own IP address space while being reachable across the underlay using provider-assigned addresses. This abstraction simplified IP management and avoided IP conflicts between tenants using overlapping address spaces.

To support routing and policy enforcement, the organization deployed Windows Server Gateway virtual machines that acted as intermediaries between the virtual networks and the physical network or the internet. These gateways handled NVGRE encapsulation for virtual machines communicating with external resources, and also performed NAT when required. Load balancing was integrated through Network Load Balancing (NLB) features in the Microsoft stack, and high availability was ensured through clustering and redundant gateway configurations. These virtual appliances allowed the organization to centralize traffic inspection, logging, and security enforcement without relying on physical network appliances.

System Center Virtual Machine Manager played a central role in orchestrating the NVGRE environment. Administrators used SCVMM to define logical networks, configure isolation policies, and assign virtual networks to specific tenants or workloads. When a virtual machine was provisioned, SCVMM automatically configured the virtual switch on the host, assigned the appropriate CA and PA addresses, and updated the mapping tables used to maintain reachability across the fabric. This automation significantly reduced the time required to onboard new tenants or scale existing applications, and it eliminated the need for manual intervention in switch configurations or IP planning.

Performance was a key concern during the design and validation phases. While NVGRE introduced some processing overhead due to the encapsulation of packets, the impact was mitigated by enabling hardware offload capabilities on the network interface cards. Hyper-V hosts equipped with Network Interface Cards that supported Virtual Machine Queue (VMQ) and single-root I/O virtualization (SR-IOV) were configured to offload NVGRE processing, allowing virtual machines to achieve near-native throughput even under high traffic loads. Performance testing was conducted using synthetic workloads that simulated typical application traffic, including database transactions, web requests, and file transfers between virtual machines across virtual networks.

Security was enforced through a combination of hypervisor-level controls and NVGRE isolation. Each virtual network operated as an independent broadcast domain, and access between networks was governed by firewall policies defined centrally through Group Policy and SCVMM templates. Role-based access controls were implemented to ensure that only authorized administrators could modify virtual network configurations. Regular audits were performed to ensure compliance with internal security policies and to verify that isolation boundaries between business units were properly maintained.

The organization also invested heavily in monitoring and troubleshooting tools to support the NVGRE environment. Microsoft System Center Operations Manager (SCOM) was extended with custom management packs to track NVGRE tunnel health, host mapping tables, and virtual network state. Integration with Windows Event Logs and Performance Monitor allowed network administrators to receive alerts on tunnel failures, high latency, or packet drops. In cases where troubleshooting was required, packet captures were taken on the Hyper-V host to inspect encapsulated traffic. Since NVGRE used standard GRE encapsulation, familiar tools like Wireshark could be used to decode and analyze the traffic, facilitating faster problem resolution.

One of the most significant benefits realized from the NVGRE deployment was increased agility. Departments that previously had to wait days or weeks for network provisioning could now deploy their own virtual networks in minutes through self-service portals integrated with SCVMM. Developers working in isolated testing environments no longer experienced IP conflicts or routing issues, and infrastructure teams were able to maintain tighter control over physical switch configurations by reducing the need for VLAN sprawl. The logical separation provided by NVGRE allowed each virtual network to evolve independently, supporting varying performance, security, and connectivity requirements without affecting others.

The NVGRE deployment also set the foundation for hybrid cloud integration. By maintaining consistent virtual network configurations on-premises, the organization was able to extend its networks into Microsoft Azure using Azure Site-to-Site VPNs and Azure Virtual Network Gateways. Virtual machines running in Azure could be configured with matching network identifiers, allowing seamless communication between cloud and on-premises workloads through NVGRE-enabled gateways. This hybrid approach enabled the enterprise to adopt a cloud-first strategy for new services without disrupting existing applications.

The case study of NVGRE in this Microsoft-centric environment demonstrates how overlay networking can deliver substantial operational benefits when aligned with the underlying platform. NVGRE allowed the organization to overcome traditional networking limitations, improve agility and scalability, and simplify the management of a large, complex virtual infrastructure. Although newer technologies such as VXLAN and GENEVE offer more advanced features, NVGRE continues to provide a viable and well-integrated solution for enterprises that rely on Microsoft's ecosystem and seek to virtualize their network infrastructure while preserving security, manageability, and control.

Case Study: GENEVE in a Cloud-Native Deployment

The adoption of cloud-native architectures has reshaped the way networks are designed, deployed, and operated. As organizations shift toward microservices, containerization, and distributed applications, traditional networking solutions often fall short in meeting the demands for agility, scalability, and rich telemetry. In this context, Generic Network Virtualization Encapsulation, or GENEVE, emerges as a next-generation overlay protocol that addresses the limitations of its predecessors by offering a highly extensible, metadata-rich framework for encapsulating and transporting network traffic in virtualized environments. This case study explores the deployment of GENEVE in a large-scale cloud-native environment built on Kubernetes, highlighting the practical benefits, architectural considerations, and operational lessons learned.

The enterprise featured in this case study is a global SaaS provider that delivers real-time data analytics services to a wide range of industries, including finance, healthcare, and retail. Its infrastructure is entirely cloud-native, relying on containerized microservices orchestrated by Kubernetes across multiple clusters hosted in both private data centers and public cloud platforms. With thousands of pods running concurrently and workloads shifting dynamically based on demand, the network needed to support high levels of isolation, low latency, efficient service discovery, and granular observability. The team initially experimented with VXLAN-based overlays but found limitations in flexibility and the lack of integrated support for rich metadata. After evaluating available alternatives, they chose to implement GENEVE as the core overlay protocol for intra-cluster and inter-cluster communication.

The GENEVE deployment was integrated into a Kubernetes-based networking stack using the Cilium CNI, which leverages eBPF to enhance networking, observability, and security in container environments. Cilium's support for GENEVE allowed for seamless encapsulation of pod traffic and introduced the ability to insert custom metadata directly into the GENEVE header. This feature proved critical for supporting service-aware routing, security enforcement, and telemetry without requiring separate infrastructure or out-of-band mechanisms. Each GENEVE packet included metadata such as service identity, security labels, and telemetry tags, enabling distributed enforcement points to make policy decisions based on this context.

One of the key benefits of GENEVE in this deployment was the ability to dynamically adapt to the needs of each microservice. Unlike traditional overlays, which have fixed header structures and limited extensibility, GENEVE supports a flexible options field that can carry an arbitrary set of metadata attributes. This allowed the team to encode service-specific data such as tenant ID, environment (development, staging, production), and application role into each packet. Policies defined in the Kubernetes network layer could then match on these attributes to allow or deny traffic, route flows to service chains, or apply quality of service tags. This flexibility aligned perfectly with the microservices model, where different services have different communication patterns, security requirements, and operational policies.

To ensure scalability, the deployment used a hierarchical design for the GENEVE overlay. Each Kubernetes node operated as a GENEVE tunnel endpoint, responsible for encapsulating and decapsulating traffic between pods and services. A distributed key-value store maintained endpoint mappings, and the Cilium agent on each node synchronized this data to ensure fast lookups and tunnel establishment. For cross-cluster communication, GENEVE tunnels were extended through gateway nodes that operated at the edge of each cluster. These gateways used the same encapsulation format and metadata schema, ensuring that service context was preserved across cluster boundaries. The unified overlay fabric supported not only pod-to-pod traffic but also integration with virtual machines and legacy workloads that were gradually being containerized.

Security was a central focus of the GENEVE-based overlay. Each packet carried a set of security labels that were derived from Kubernetes pod annotations and service accounts. These labels were interpreted by eBPF programs running in the kernel, which enforced fine-grained policies such as allowlist rules, rate limits, and deep inspection. Because the labels were part of the GENEVE header, enforcement could occur immediately upon decapsulation without requiring additional lookups or delays. The security team developed automated pipelines to validate and deploy policy changes, ensuring that new services inherited the correct enforcement rules from day one. Additionally, the use of GENEVE allowed for in-band telemetry collection, capturing performance metrics such as latency, packet loss, and hop count as the packets traversed the network.

Observability was one of the most impactful outcomes of the GENEVE deployment. By embedding telemetry metadata directly in the GENEVE headers, the team was able to build a real-time analytics platform that visualized traffic patterns, service dependencies, and network health across the entire fabric. This platform integrated with Grafana, Prometheus, and OpenTelemetry to provide rich dashboards and alerts. Engineers could trace the journey of any packet through the system, see which services it interacted with, and diagnose issues such as bottlenecks, dropped packets, or policy violations. This observability also fed into automated remediation workflows, where alerts triggered rollbacks, traffic rerouting, or scaling actions.

Performance tuning was an essential aspect of the deployment. The team conducted extensive benchmarking to measure the overhead introduced by GENEVE encapsulation, particularly when combined with eBPF processing. Optimizations included the use of XDP for early packet processing, CPU pinning to reduce cache contention, and leveraging smart NICs capable of offloading encapsulation tasks. These efforts ensured that the network could handle high throughput and low latency requirements even under peak load conditions. The combination of GENEVE and eBPF delivered near line-rate performance while maintaining programmability and visibility, a balance that was previously difficult to achieve.

Over time, the GENEVE overlay became a foundational element of the organization's infrastructure strategy. It supported blue-green deployments by enabling traffic splitting based on metadata, allowed service chains to be dynamically constructed without reconfiguring the physical network, and simplified disaster recovery through seamless rerouting between active and standby clusters. The team began to use GENEVE's extensibility for emerging use cases such as zero trust networking, where identity and trust scores were embedded in packet headers and evaluated by enforcement points at each hop.

The deployment of GENEVE in this cloud-native environment highlighted the power of a protocol designed for modern workloads. It demonstrated that encapsulation is no longer just about segmentation but also about context, observability, and adaptability. By leveraging GENEVE's extensible architecture, the organization was able to build a network that was deeply integrated with their services, responsive to change, and transparent to operators. This case study serves as a blueprint for future-facing networking strategies that embrace complexity not by adding layers of rigidity but by enabling layers of intelligent abstraction and control.

The Future of Overlay Networking

Overlay networking has become a cornerstone of modern network architecture, enabling flexibility, scalability, and isolation in ways that traditional networking cannot match. As organizations continue their journey toward cloud-native applications, hybrid cloud infrastructures, and edge computing, overlay networking is poised to evolve further, adapting to new demands and embracing innovations in automation, observability, and programmability. The future of overlay networking lies not just in providing connectivity but in embedding intelligence, context, and policy into every packet and every path. This evolution will reshape how networks are designed, operated, and consumed.

The driving forces behind the continued development of overlay networking are rooted in the ever-increasing complexity of distributed systems. Applications are no longer confined to monolithic servers or single locations. They are composed of hundreds or thousands of microservices, deployed across diverse environments including private data centers, public clouds, and edge nodes. These services must communicate reliably and securely, regardless of where they are hosted or how they move. Overlay networks solve this by abstracting the physical infrastructure and presenting a unified, programmable connectivity layer that can adapt in real time to changes in application topology, load, and policy requirements.

One of the most significant trends shaping the future of overlay networking is the integration of intent-based networking principles. Intent-based systems allow administrators to define high-level business goals, such as security policies or service availability targets, while the network automatically translates these intents into low-level configurations. In overlay networks, this means dynamically provisioning tunnels, enforcing segmentation, applying quality-of-service rules, and rerouting traffic based on current conditions and defined intent. The overlay fabric becomes a self-adjusting entity that ensures compliance and performance without requiring constant manual oversight. With the support of machine learning algorithms and real-time telemetry, intent-based overlays will be able to anticipate needs, detect anomalies, and self-correct before issues impact users.

Programmability is another defining feature of the future overlay landscape. Technologies such as eBPF, P4, and programmable data planes are opening new possibilities for in-network computation, custom telemetry, and adaptive security enforcement. Overlay protocols like GENEVE, which support extensible metadata, will play a critical role in enabling programmable overlays. Metadata embedded in encapsulation headers will carry information about application identity, user context, trust level, and traffic classification, allowing enforcement points to make decisions based on rich, context-aware policies. This level of granularity and adaptability will be essential in environments where services are ephemeral and users are mobile.

Security will continue to be a dominant theme in overlay networking's evolution. As threats become more sophisticated and distributed, networks must evolve to become zero trust by design. Overlay networks will embed security context directly into the data plane, supporting end-to-end encryption, mutual authentication, and dynamic policy enforcement. Every packet will carry evidence of its identity and purpose, and every hop will have the means to verify and enforce policies accordingly. Overlay-enabled microsegmentation will go beyond static rules, adapting to workload behavior and network conditions in real time. Security services such as intrusion detection, deep packet inspection, and anomaly detection will be distributed throughout the overlay, operating as virtualized or containerized functions that scale with demand.

Another key development in overlay networking is its convergence with service mesh architectures. Service meshes provide fine-grained control over service-to-service communication, offering features such as retries, load balancing, encryption, and observability at the application layer. By integrating with or building upon overlay networks, service meshes will gain deeper control over the network path, allowing for optimized routing, enhanced telemetry, and coordinated policy enforcement across layers. The fusion of overlay networking and service mesh will enable consistent security, routing, and observability from the kernel to the application, across any infrastructure.

The edge computing paradigm will also influence the future of overlays. As data generation shifts toward the edge, networks must extend their capabilities beyond centralized data centers to geographically distributed nodes with limited resources and intermittent connectivity. Overlay networks will become lightweight and resilient, capable of maintaining service continuity across flaky links and dynamically adjusting to changing network topologies. Edge overlays will prioritize minimal latency, localized processing, and data sovereignty, while still integrating with centralized management and policy frameworks. Technologies such as peer-to-peer tunneling, adaptive path selection, and distributed service registries will become standard components of overlay architectures designed for edge deployments.

Automation and orchestration will be central to managing the increasing complexity of overlay networks. Infrastructure as code, CI/CD pipelines, and automated policy engines will be used to provision, monitor, and update overlay components in real time. Overlays will integrate with cloud management platforms, container orchestrators, and network controllers to ensure that changes in application state are instantly reflected in the network. This automation will enable developers to treat the network as a service, abstracting away the intricacies of routing and security and allowing them to focus on application logic. DevSecOps principles will drive the convergence of network, security, and application workflows, with overlay networks acting as the glue that binds them together.

Observability will evolve from passive monitoring to active feedback. Overlay networks will continuously measure their own performance, emitting rich telemetry that describes not only what is happening but why. Correlated metrics across overlay and underlay, integrated with application logs and business outcomes, will provide a holistic view of system health. Anomalies will be detected in real time, and remediations will be automated based on policy and machine learning.

This shift will reduce mean time to resolution, support proactive optimization, and provide assurance for service-level agreements.

Interoperability will also be a focus area as organizations adopt multi-cloud and hybrid architectures. Overlay networks must span different administrative domains, encapsulation formats, and policy models. Standardization efforts around protocols such as GENEVE, integration with BGP EVPN, and adoption of open APIs will be necessary to ensure that overlays can bridge clouds, data centers, and edge locations without fragmentation. The future will demand overlays that are not only powerful and flexible but also open, portable, and vendor-agnostic.

Overlay networking is transitioning from a tool for network abstraction to a platform for intelligent, context-aware, and policy-driven communication. Its future lies in its ability to integrate with every layer of the infrastructure stack, from silicon to software, and to enable new levels of agility, security, and insight. As the digital landscape continues to expand in scale and complexity, overlay networking will evolve to meet it, not by simplifying the complexity, but by mastering it through programmability, automation, and intelligence. The networks of tomorrow will not just connect endpoints; they will understand them, protect them, and adapt to them in ways that are only beginning to emerge. Overlay networking is not a transitional architecture; it is the foundation upon which future infrastructure will be built.

Conclusion and Final Thoughts

Overlay networking has become one of the most significant innovations in the evolution of modern network architecture, fundamentally altering how connectivity, segmentation, and scalability are approached in complex, distributed environments. What began as a solution to the limitations of traditional VLAN-based networking in virtualized data centers has grown into a comprehensive framework that powers everything from cloud-native applications and multi-tenant platforms to hybrid cloud architectures and global service delivery models. Throughout this book, we have examined the core concepts, technologies, protocols, and real-world applications that define overlay networking today, and in doing so, we have uncovered the key patterns that will continue to shape its development for years to come.

At its core, overlay networking is about abstraction. By decoupling logical network constructs from the physical infrastructure beneath them, overlays allow networks to become more agile, responsive, and programmable. This abstraction is not merely a convenience; it is a necessity in a world where workloads can be instantiated, moved, scaled, and decommissioned in seconds across infrastructure that spans continents. Overlay protocols such as VXLAN, NVGRE, and GENEVE provide the encapsulation mechanisms that make this abstraction possible, allowing Layer 2 and Layer 3 connectivity to be stretched across diverse IP fabrics without relying on traditional broadcast domains or manual configuration. These protocols serve as the foundation for scalable, resilient network fabrics that can support the demands of modern application architectures.

Beyond their encapsulation capabilities, overlay networks have proven to be powerful tools for enforcing security and segmentation. The ability to create logically isolated environments within the same physical infrastructure has enabled multi-tenancy at scale, empowered zero trust security models, and reduced the risk of lateral movement in the event of a breach. Microsegmentation, enabled by overlays and often enhanced by integration with container platforms and orchestration tools, has become a cornerstone of modern security strategies. The metadata carried within overlay headers allows for granular policy enforcement, contextual traffic steering, and visibility that was previously impossible with conventional networking tools.

Scalability is another defining feature of overlay networking. Traditional VLANs are constrained by a hard limit of 4096 identifiers, a limitation that becomes unacceptable in large data centers or cloud environments supporting many tenants or applications. VXLAN alone increases the identifier space to over 16 million segments, and GENEVE extends this even further by allowing virtually limitless customization through extensible metadata. This scalability is not only about quantity; it is about the ability to manage complexity. Overlay networks are designed to grow organically, adapting to the evolving needs of applications and users without requiring fundamental redesigns or hardware upgrades.

Automation and orchestration have also become inseparable from overlay network deployments. As infrastructure becomes code and operations shift toward DevOps and GitOps models, the network must be as programmable and dynamic as the workloads it supports. Overlay networks have embraced this shift by offering APIs, integration with orchestration platforms, and support for declarative configuration models. Tools like Ansible, Terraform, and Kubernetes-native networking plugins make it possible to define and deploy overlay networks as part of continuous integration and delivery pipelines. This level of automation enables faster deployment times, consistent configurations, and reduced human error, all while supporting the speed and agility required by modern development teams.

Observability has emerged as a critical requirement in overlay networking, and it is an area where tremendous progress continues to be made. Overlay traffic, by nature, obscures the original packet headers and can make traditional monitoring tools ineffective. To address this, overlay protocols now support in-band telemetry, metadata tagging, and integration with advanced analytics platforms. Operators can trace flows across overlay and underlay, detect anomalies in real time, and correlate performance metrics with application behavior. This depth of insight is essential for maintaining service levels, identifying root causes, and optimizing the network for both efficiency and user experience.

Overlay networking is not without its challenges. The added complexity of encapsulation, control plane design, and multi-layer troubleshooting can introduce steep learning curves and operational hurdles. However, with the right tools, practices, and training, these challenges are surmountable. The evolution of controllers, observability platforms, and intelligent automation is steadily closing the gap between complexity and manageability. As overlay networks become more integrated with intent-based systems and artificial intelligence, the burden on human operators will continue to decrease, allowing them to focus on higher-level strategy and design rather than day-to-day configuration and debugging.

One of the most exciting aspects of overlay networking is its ability to serve as a unifying platform across different types of infrastructure. Whether in the data center, across public clouds, or at the network edge, overlays provide a consistent connectivity fabric that abstracts away heterogeneity and enforces a coherent policy framework. This ability to bridge gaps, integrate technologies, and deliver services end-to-end is what makes overlay networking not just a tactical solution, but a strategic enabler. It supports the creation of hybrid and multi-cloud architectures that deliver flexibility without sacrificing control, and it enables distributed applications to operate with the same security and performance guarantees regardless of where they run.

Looking ahead, overlay networking will continue to evolve in tandem with the broader trends in computing. The rise of edge computing, the proliferation of IoT devices, the push toward AI-driven operations, and the demands of real-time applications will all place new requirements on the network. Overlay technologies will rise to meet these challenges by becoming more lightweight, more intelligent, and more deeply integrated into the infrastructure stack. Encapsulation will no longer be just a transport mechanism; it will become a vehicle for carrying identity, policy, and context throughout the network, enabling new levels of automation, security, and insight.

Ultimately, overlay networking is more than a set of protocols or configurations. It is a paradigm shift in how networks are built, managed, and consumed. It reflects the broader transformation of IT from static infrastructure to dynamic, service-oriented architecture. It empowers organizations to deliver secure, scalable, and high-performing connectivity wherever it is needed, with the agility to adapt to any future state. For network architects, engineers, and operators, mastering overlay networking is no longer optional—it is essential. As this technology continues to mature, it will define the fabric of modern infrastructure, enabling the next generation of innovation across industries and use cases. Overlay networking is not just a tool for today; it is the foundation of the networks of tomorrow.

www.ingramcontent.com/pod-product-compliance
Lightning Source LLC
LaVergne TN
LVHW051234050326
832903LV00028B/2401